GW00320040

HOW TO BE AN EFFECTIVE FATHER

How To Be
an Effective Father

Ian Grant

KINGSWAY PUBLICATIONS
EASTBOURNE

Published by
KINGSWAY COMMUNICATIONS LTD
Lottbridge Drove, Eastbourne BN23 6NT, England.
Email: books@kingsway.co.uk

Cover design and book production for the publishers by
Bookprint Creative Services, P.O. Box 827, BN21 3YJ, England.
Printed in Great Britain.

DEDICATION

I would like to thank my wife Mary for her contribution to this book. I am grateful for her many skills, intelligence and beauty; she is an awesome lady.

I would like to thank my family and their spouses:
Andrew and Elle; Kim and Craig; Jonathan and Esther – they have taught me heaps about fatherhood. I'm honoured to be their Dad.

I would like to thank my colleague John Cowan for his inspiration, "off-the-wall" thinking and humour. What is life without laughter?

Finally, I would like to thank the many mentors – too many to name – who have influenced my life. Thank you all.

Ian Grant

CONTENTS

Lifeskills

FOREWORD

As we enter the new millennium, unity within families is at an all time crisis. In the modern world, fathers and mothers are being forced to give in to the pressures of living in an extremely materialistic and complex society.

The overused cliche 'if it feels good do it' is fast becoming a common excuse for letting things slide. The responsibility banner has been lowered and the self banner has been erected.

The principles of love, honour and integrity are vital ingredients in any successful relationship. But with future generations growing up in divided homes, we are not always giving our children the ideal family structure to lay a secure foundation for later life.

As a father myself of three gorgeous children, and as a husband of nine years, I too, have experienced the dilemmas and joys of parenthood. Being a husband and father is one of the most character-building jobs any man can have. To know that you are a person responsible for your children's growth is frightening, and when you think about the complex nature of modern society, it can be bewildering.

In spite of fatherhood's obvious challenges, it is with great delight that I pen this foreword for Ian Grant's book. We live in a day when the need to equip ourselves with wisdom and knowledge about what a good father looks like, is beyond any doubt. Ian Grant has done us a wonderful service. For this book is filled with an imaginative stock of life-giving wisdom.

In searching for information on how to be a good father myself, I have found no greater help than in knowing the Almighty Father in heaven. God has given me my greatest paradigm for parenting.

Nevertheless, I also need the example of men who have successfully mastered the task. For sheer good fun and inspiring ideas on fatherhood, Ian Grant can be a mentor to us all.

Each day I watch my children studying me as I set them on a path and give them boundaries for the future. The early years of building relationships with them will have profound effects on their lives. The only way that I know to build a lasting friendship with my kids is to put time into it.

To make time for my family is an issue of setting priorities. These priorities must be reviewed on a regular basis, and only when this has happened can I be certain of meeting my family's needs.

In being a jockey, and in winning a few races throughout my 17 year career, I eventually got to know what it takes to make a success of life. I discovered that there are no short cuts to success, and I am sure as a father of three that the same is true of parenting. I have to work at it, keep learn-ing, keep improving.

Therefore I wholeheartedly and unreservedly endorse Ian Grant's book. It is written in plain, uncomplicated English. And by making the time to read, reflect upon, and under-stand Ian's many practical strategies, I know that fathers throughout the world will succeed and raise wonderful, hope-filled children.

It is my prayer that Ian's book accomplishes its stated aim—to dare us all to be winning, effective dads.

Darren J. Beadman

Dual-Melbourne-Cup Winning Jockey
TV and Media Commentator on Racing

INTRODUCTION

Parentage is a very important profession; but no test of fitness for it is ever imposed in the interests of children – G.B. Shaw

Once a parent, always a parent. While the demands of parenting change as sons and daughters grow, parents cannot escape their lot – being Mum or Dad – throughout the rest of their lives. There is no warrant of fitness, no qualifying examination or syllabus, other than one's own childhood experiences and natural maternal and paternal instincts. These experiences and instincts vary enormously from person to person and are shaped by so many variables. First and foremost one's own parents, then a vast range of other influences such as family size, cultural background, friends, schooling, rural or urban life and the pressures of time.

Surely most parents try, but all of us could benefit from some extra help along the way. We often lack the confidence and know-how, the time, the inspiration and an awareness of the issues that really matter, to enable us to enjoy family. By the time you might be able to be good at it, you are more likely to be a grandparent!

Parenting has always been a challenge, with each generation having to cope with different demanding issues. Perhaps the 1990s have placed greater stress on the family unit than ever before. There have been changing attitudes to the sanctity of marriage and the consequent break up of families, society's permissiveness towards differing lifestyles, a neglect of the Christian ethic, uncertain economic times and a growing number of unemployed and unemployable. Add to these the effect of written and visual media, which highlight the trivial, are often so negative and frequently seem to present as role models those who exhibit extremes of behaviour. All these have put immense pressures on adults and young people alike.

Ian Grant recognises the pressures and takes sound principles and practices of parenting, and with an optimism and enthusiasm presents a refreshing approach to the challenges of family life. Ian has an unshakeable belief in the goodness of people and believes that much of that is untapped. He sees united, happy, positive families as vital to the wellbeing of national life. He sees dads as having a far more critical role to play in the growth of a family and the personal development of each child than many would believe.

He carefully defines the role of dad in the family. There is no jargon, no preaching; just a positive and encouraging approach to the many parts a dad must play. Some could see his style as light-hearted but he never trivialises or underestimates the challenges he knows dads face daily. He dares all dads to accept and enjoy his challenge. Having got the essential message across, he interlaces it with good humour, whimsical tales and enough variations to suit dads of all shapes and sizes. His practical suggestions are within everyone's grasp.

As a grandparent with all the wisdom of hindsight, I have had my failures and triumphs exposed through Ian Grant's remarkable skill. I did not feel bruised or diminished, but I am delighted for modern fathers who will enjoy using Ian Grant's wisdom and experience to enhance their own and their families' lives.

Ian Grant has always had a wonderfully positive approach, presented with flair, good humour and a warm understanding of people's strengths and weaknesses. There is too, always a clear message founded on a significant principle. Ian Grant reminds us all that fathers who dare, win.

D. John Graham

Captain, New Zealand 'All Blacks' Rugby Team, 1964
Headmaster, Auckland Grammar School, 1973-93
Manager, New Zealand Cricket Team, 1996-

AUTHOR'S INTRODUCTION

Like coming out of a painful nightmare, suddenly our society is waking up to how important fathers are in raising their kids. This has happened because we are now coming face to face with the results of large numbers of children being brought up without a dad in their lives. Angry, unattached young men, acting out violently and without conscience and young girls looking for male love and affirmation in inappropriate ways, paint a picture of children who lack fathers.

Today's world desperately needs men who are not just generous at conception; it needs committed men who are generous in the fathering of their offspring; not just baby makers, but creative dads who will hang in there with their kids through the good times and the tough times.

Fathers, we need to reclaim our manhood, leaving a legacy of great fathering for the next generation through our actions and our investments now.

The greatest legacy a man can leave in the world is not so much a great business, but a "living" investment in the future, through loving, stable, employable and healthy children. Parents are the ultimate "people-builders". The fine expectations you have of your children, the skills you teach them, and the values you model for them will be the bricks and mortar of great future citizens.

History very rarely records a businessman on his deathbed wishing he had spent more time at the office! The usual dying wish is that he had spent more time with his family. Despite this, it is amazing how many men let the unique opportunity to be a mentor and friend to their children slip by.

Successful fathering may demand energy; it may even require drawing on those inner reserves; but if you see the challenge of fathering as the biggest victory of your life, it will be a goal worth stretching for.

My aim in writing this book is to encourage Dads to realise their potential in making a difference to their children's lives. Today's tragedy is that the "tyranny of the urgent" often overwhelms men with a maelstrom of meetings, deadlines and commitments which all scream out for priority attention. Men get caught up in careers, sport and other perfectly fine things, while the most important thing in life—being a father—may receive a low priority, even if just by default. We live in a world where work, meetings, schedules, budgets, the pressures to pay the mortgage, the credit card or the school fees, are always present.

But it is just a question of priorities. If you see your children as the most important investment opportunity you have, and want to capitalise on the window of opportunity that their childhood offers, then this book is for you.

In January 1990 I found myself lying on the ground somewhere in the Malborough Sounds, having just survived a
light plane crash. It was one of the truly focussing moments
of my life.

I remember being interviewed on television news afterwards. The reporter had heard, as I had, of stories of people whose whole lives flashed before them as they believed
they faced death. He asked me what flashed through my
mind in those seconds as we dropped out of the sky. All I
could remember thinking at that moment, as the stalled
engine screamed and we fell to the ground, was, 'Flip! those
wings are short!'

But I do clearly remember lying on the ground after being
rescued and having all my "vitals"—my eyebrows, toes, fin-
gers and crown jewels—checked out! The police sergeant
who arrived on the scene, recognised me and asked, 'What
are you doing here?' To which I replied 'I'm just getting a
real life illustration for my talks.' He quipped, 'You were
very nearly someone else's illustration!'

However as I lay there being prodded by the medics and
feeling very sore, my life did suddenly come into clear
focus. Not my whole life - just the most important parts. I
felt as if I was looking at myself through a telephoto lens
and there were only two things in the shot —my family and
my God! Everything else was completely out of focus.

When it came to the crunch (literally!) nothing else made
it into the picture. Not my new car or my collection of
power tools, not any past achievements or future plans. It
was as if the crisis of the accident had focused me on true

reality—what really counted in life. At that moment, the web of family relationships and memories that made up my life were the only reality.

I can honestly say that fatherhood has been the greatest pleasure of my life. Not because I have been the greatest dad in the world, but because my children have developed a maturity in me that would have been impossible without their unique personalities.

The innocence and earnestness of my three-year-old son who asked 'Why Dad?' a hundred times a day, drew out in me a protectiveness that was deep and fierce. My small daughter's brokenheartedness every morning as I left for work, stunned me with the knowledge that this two-year-old's world revolved around her connection to her mother and me, and that my comings and goings mattered to her. During the teenage years, my kids both challenged and indulged me. They called me to account when I needed it, but they loved me unconditionally and warmly.

As our children have grown to young adulthood I watched them hammer out their beliefs around the dinner table and test their character in the marketplace. I feel truly grateful, as I enjoy the company of the warm, interesting human beings my children have become. I certainly consider my investment in their childhood to be the best decision of my life. I am humbled by the pleasure I receive as I watch each make their own positive contribution to the world. Fatherhood is definitely the most challenging, "grown up" thing I've ever done.

I hope that this book helps you towards a similar outcome.

And I hope that you can grab some of the following strategies, even on your busiest days, and enjoy the time of your life, parenting your family.

EFFECTIVE FATHERS IN THE NEW MILLENNIUM

The best way I can express the job description for a Dad in the modern world is through the term "parent coach". A coach sees the individual strengths of his players and while affirming and challenging each one, inspires them to become a co-operative part of a winning team. Most of all a good coach stays on his pedestal and, through his belief in his players, wins their respect and love.

I recently heard that my adult son took part in a major debate (at Monash university in Melbourne), on the subject of leadership and its potential use for good or evil. He closed his speech with a story I had told him when he was a child.

The story was about a farming community that had gathered together for harvest. At the end of a tiring day, as they were packing up, they realised that a small boy was missing. For hours, in the darkness, they looked for him, but without success. Next morning at first light, they began searching again. This time, an old farmer suggested that they all join hands and comb the fields. They soon found the little boy, but he had died of exposure during the night. His distraught mother cried out, "If only we'd joined hands sooner!"

Fathers have the ability to join hands with their wives and their children to make their family a place where children gain security, significance (the sense that their ideas are valuable) and self-esteem.

Research about families and children tells us that a father influences his children in many ways, including:

- ❂ The intellectual ability of his children.
- ❂ The behaviour his children will model.
- ❂ The occupational choices his children make.
- ❂ The material resources his children are left with when he is gone.
- ❂ The attitudes his children will hold regarding their children.
- ❂ The memories his children will have after he dies or separates from the family.

(from Ken Canfield "Seven Secrets of Effective Fathers" Wheaton: Tyndale 1992)

When spelled out like this, it is sobering to think about the power we fathers have over our children's future.

I regularly speak at high school assemblies and am saddened by how often the principal, after thanking me, comments that the biggest problem the school faces is boys whose fathers aren't there for them. He usually goes on to say something like, 'We thought that having an absent father would affect girls more, but we have found that it deeply affects boys. In fact, just about every problem boy here, has a father who is not there for him.'

When you look at the research conducted on father absence, a number of key issues keep coming up. These are:

- ✪ The impact of an absent father is greater on the male child than the female child.
- ✪ The impact of father absence can be seen in both personality and cognition, particularly in boys.
- ✪ The age at which separation occurs seems to be crucial (before age 5 having the greatest effect).
- ✪ The feminising effects of male absence on a male child can be mitigated if male figures are available to him.

There is also research on the effect of an absent father on girls. Feminine behaviour in a girl seems to relate to how her father

- ✪ Defines his role, as a male, to his daughter.
- ✪ Differentiates his masculine role from her feminine role.

I have a vivid picture in my mind of a little boy in an episode of 'The Oprah Winfrey Show,' dedicated to children. Children from many different ethnic groups had been interviewed about their parents. Most had giggled and enthusiastically said things like:

'My Dad is always there to encourage me. Even when I don't do things very well, he still says that I was good.'

'When my sister and I fight, my Dad explains that we need to learn to work things out, because your sister should be your friend.'

The programme kept returning to a cute, but sad, little boy who had never known a father. The final question to this little guy was, 'What would you like to say to your dad if you ever met him?'

He replied, 'I'd like to say to him, *Where have you been all these years?*'

This little guy summed up for me the "father hunger" that so many children today feel. The tragedy of our society is that in the last fifty years we have underestimated the role of a good dad in the family.

Thank you for reading this book. It may be the first step towards you making a difference in your own life and in your children's lives; and there may also be spin-off blessings for any of your children's friends who are desperately looking for father role models. You can be a "light on a hill" to children who are watching your family and who long to break the dysfunctional family cycle.

FATHERS HOLD THE FUTURE IN THEIR HANDS

The investment a father makes in his children's lives pays definite dividends in their physical, social, mental and spiritual development. When a father sees himself as a coach, he will make sure that his team members have, what I like to call the building blocks of life.

A father who brings the 'Aa-aa-h!' factor into his home is a father who wins. Our children need us to cheer and clap for them—encouraging praising and honouring them. For instance, a father who arrives home and calls out 'Where are the most awesome kids in the world?' will have little toddlers rushing to the door saying 'Here I am Daddy, Here I am!' Even a cynical teenager may grunt a response after being called 'awesome!'

The building blocks of life are simple:

- ✪   Give your children a variety of experiences when they are small. This will develop their brain power. If you sing and dance with your toddlers, let them feel a fluffy chicken or feed a lamb and read stories with them, your children's brains will form the connections they need. It is these early experiences encouraged and supervised by you, that are the building blocks of intelligence, creativity and autonomy.

- ✪   Establish consistent love and limits. This will give them the security they need. Your panicky two-year-old will feel secure when you quietly make him stand and think about what he should do. He will learn to sequence his thoughts, rather than scramble them.

- ✪   Teach your children skills and let them practise doing things with you. This will build their self-esteem. Your seven-year-old will value not only the toys he helped you build, but also the time spent with you, learning to be a man.

- ✪   Put dreams into your children's heads. This will give them a future. Arthur Lydiard, the great athletics coach, who took ordinary neighbourhood boys and made them into world champions, never said to them, 'You could be a New Zealand champion,' He said, 'You could be a world champion.'

Remember there is an additional pay off; the creative children you have a hand in developing, will be the ones who are likely to choose the retirement home in which you spend the last stretch of your life!

You may remember the messages your parents handed on to you. The negative ones may have stuck with you and may still affect your view of yourself. Things like:
'You clumsy Clot.'
'Idiot.'
'You'll never amount to anything.'

Or maybe there were positive ones, like:
'Respect yourself.'
'You can do it.'
'Winners never quit.'
'You may sometimes suffer defeat, but you don't ever have to be defeated.'
'Things don't always have to go right for me to be happy.'

We have the power in our words to leave good, energising and healing messages in our children's heads and thus ensure their future. It will be their beliefs that determine their attitudes and actions.

Messages such as the following will mould a child's view of his own ability as well as his values:

- ✪ 'There's no problem so big that it can't be solved.'
- ✪ 'You're a helpful person.'
- ✪ 'Tough times don't last, but tough people do.'
- ✪ 'You make friends easily.'
- ✪ 'Honesty is the best policy.'
- ✪ 'Mistakes are OK. Mistakes can be fixed.'
- ✪ 'The person who never made a mistake never made anything.'

QUALITIES THAT AFFECT CHILDREN

When a father offers his children safety and security he fosters trust. If you are a father who is fair, firm and friendly, you will be your child's first hero. There are times when little children will ask you impossible questions, like 'Dad how many leaves are there on that tree?' It's fun to give wild answers. It's fun to say, 'It looks to me that there are about 63,433. Oops one just fell off—63,432!' In a strange way little kids love dads who know things like that.

Children need you to be their hero. The one they can trust—the one they can go to, with the stuff they feel too small to handle. They need you to know more than they do and to teach them what you know.

SONS

Your sons will relate to you strongly in the years between ages six and ten. They are learning what it is to be a boy and are male-role-model- seeking-missiles during those years. Capitalise on their desire to please and their belief in your hero status.

They will need you again at puberty to initiate them into manhood. They may push you away as they look for their own identity and try to establish their individuality, but your role as mentor is vital. If you have spent time building a comradeship with them in the early years, that will see you through the time when they are breaking away and establishing their independence. Your task is to gently push them towards linking choices with consequences and learning to take responsibility for their own actions.

DAUGHTERS

Your daughters will draw much of their self-esteem and the way they see themselves from your view of them. You are the first man in your daughter's life and probably the most influential. Absent or involved, loving or rejecting, you will leave a lasting imprint. Your daughter will need your affirmation; you will be the 'safe' male on whom she can practise conversation and mutual admiration. Be involved with your daughters. Admire them; teach them self-sufficiency. Respect their space, and be careful never to evaluate their looks except positively.

HOW FATHERS DIFFER FROM MOTHERS

Understanding some fundamental differences between men and women is vital to realising your own value as a father in the family.

A man has great strengths, and his contribution to the family is very different from a mother's. Generally speaking, men tend to see in 'spotlight', whereas a woman will see things more in floodlight. For instance, mothers seem to be able to cook the dinner, while answering the phone and dealing with the children's problems. We men like to concentrate on one thing only. When we are cooking the barbeque, it is our focus of attention and we will concentrate on that one thing. Apparently it has to do with how our brains were structured, even before we were born. Men's brains are wired in such a way that we open one file at a time and work on it, then close it and open another, whereas women have the ability to have heaps of files open at the same time and be able to keep track of most of what is in them. However we men do have one great strength: If we are given a plan, we will usually make it happen. Consequently, in writing this book, I have tried to keep the chapters short and the strategies in the form of plans.

The great strengths of a man are that:

- ✪   When you give him a plan, he will make it happen.
- ✪   He will be loyal to those who believe in him

The great strengths of a woman are that:

- ✪   She will work to make meaningful relationships happen.
- ✪   She can evaluate meaningful relationships.

What a great team men and women make when they parent together! As this book is for men, I will focus on the qualities of a father in the relationship. However, God is kind — most of us sleep with a relationship expert! Don't ignore this gift; allow your partner to advise you in those areas in which you may lack insight.

A major company was researching how men see themselves and what motivates them. They discovered that men identified with images of themselves as:

- ✪   Heroes
- ✪   Fathers
- ✪   Lovers
- ✪   Sportsmen
- ✪   Businessmen
- ✪   Toolmen
- ✪   Mentors

It is significant that we men identify with the roles of sportsmen, heroes, lovers, mentors, providers and protectors. I believe that these are the roles for which we are naturally suited and, I suggest those are the very roles in which we are most needed today as fathers.

Fathers leave an indelible imprint on their children. This tends to show up in what we remember of our father's words and actions from our childhood. When a daughter has a dad who teaches her how to ride her first bicycle, who takes her places with him, who acts the fool and reads stories, she is likely to grow into a young woman who enjoys challenges and believes that she can achieve her goals. A son who remembers his father trusting him with an adult task is likely to use initiative and creativity as he rises to fulfil the positive expectations of his father.

WHY I WROTE THIS BOOK

I have read many books about fathering and it is great to see them in the marketplace. However, my suspicion is that not many men read them. If they do, transferring the theory into practical ideas is not always easy. I am convinced that most men have an innate desire to be good fathers, but with the jungle of media and societal messages, many of us have lost our way and our creativity. I also know that we live in a real world of deadlines and demands on our time.

We fathers don't always have the time to read a long book of theory. Therefore I hope the format of user-friendly, bite-sized strategies will be a tool to make family life smoother and help build great relationships between dads and their children in the new millennium.

I have always been drawn to books about the S.A.S. because of their tradition of courage, honour and compassion – the best ideals of manhood. The qualities of S.A.S. trained men are interesting. Each man is an expert in many specialities, but he operates with high personal discipline and team-work.

- He doesn't flaunt his leadership. He doesn't wear epaulettes to declare his authority; he has earned it.
- He doesn't use a 'scatter gun' approach, but uses his skills and equipment wisely.
- He never brags about his position or achievements, but is quietly confident he's done a good job.
- He rates zero per cent on the "BS" scale. He clearly knows where reality ends and fantasy starts.
- He knows who is running the show, where the buck stops.
- He has the guts to improve where he is weak.
- He is proactive when action is needed to address a difficult task.

These, I believe, are great qualities for a dad, too.

A STRATEGY FOR BEING
A HERO TO YOUR KIDS

Never give in, never give in, never, never, never—in nothing great or small, large or petty—never give in except to convictions of honour and good sense.

Winston Churchill, Harrow School, 29 October 1941

I wanted to be just like him, except for the drug habit, the failed marriages, the temper and the guns.

Daman Wayans, comedian roasting Richard Pryor, who won the first Mark Twain Prize for Humour, Time Magazine, November 1998

A STRATEGY FOR BEING
A HERO TO YOUR KIDS

✪ Be committed for the long haul.
✪ Focus on your children's world —not just on your own.
✪ Be available.
✪ Invest in experiences, not things.
✪ Be a hero to your children's friends.
✪ Hug your children often.
✪ Value them—not just their performance.
✪ Teach your children to compete with, not against, each other. (The former breeds team spirit, the latter sibling rivalry.)

Not many of us have the opportunity to rush into a burning building, while being shot at by terrorists, to rescue a damsel in distress. However our children need their dads to be heroes. Our children need moral heroes, faithful heroes, and wise heroes. Heroes who will honour their pledges and commitments even when the going gets tough; who will hang in there with their kids long after there is any reward in it for them.

In fiction, heroes are born on Krypton and possess super-human ability to do the things they do. The stories of real-life heroes show that they are normally cut from common cloth and possess all the frailty and fears common to us all. However when needed, they are there for those who need protection or rescuing.

As a father, you have an advantage; you don't have to do anything superhuman—you already are a hero to your kids (until they discover otherwise!). Until about the age of twelve, unless you are very unlucky, your children will probably think you are the best father they could ever have. After that, a radical re-evaluation may take place! Relax, because the word 'teenager' is not a disease; it is just a time of life, and there will still be many instances when even your teenagers need the "hero" dad to be there for them.

I like this story, told to me by a friend, about how his teenage daughter rang him one night from a party. He picked up the phone and before he could say anything, she said, 'Oh Dad, do I have to come home now? It's only 11 o'clock! Oh Dad! Oh! All right, do you know where to come? OK, I'll be out on the street in 10 minutes.' He hadn't said a word yet! But he understood the message—his daughter didn't want to be where she was; she wanted a safe (and face-saving) 'out' of the situation, and she knew she could use her father as the fall guy! He said, 'I drove to pick her up feeling like James Bond!' He was her knight in shining armour; someone she knew she could trust to be there when she needed him.

If you were to ask a group of children who their heroes were, you might get answers such as The Spice Girls, Michael Jackson, or perhaps Jonah Lomu. But true heroes are not media personalities or pop stars. Parents are the logical ones to be heroes to their kids.

True heroes are there for the long haul. Fathers who demonstrate character, kindness, consistency and integrity—are the most inspiring role models and true heroes. Children of these sort of fathers are "boomerang" kids. They keep coming back! Remember the song 'Cats in the Cradle'. The son kept repeating, 'I want to be like you Dad' and in the end that is just who he became, but in a sad negative way!

✪   True heroes are never too big to bend down to help others.

❂   True heroes can combine strength and gentleness.
❂   True heroes never become so used to succeeding
        that they can't remember what it feels like to fail.

The concept of a family as a team is so important. All of us want to be in the winning team—if not the winning team, then a fun team that has dependable boundaries and wants us as a member. Basically we need to matter. That need for significance is one of our most important human needs.

One of the ways we can communicate significance is to develop the habit of story-telling. Fathers play a vital role in extending and challenging their children. When your children ask a 'Why Dad?' sort of question, reply with a story. Create a special story for each child; their own adventure, with them as the hero, in which they carry out brave and wonderful exploits. I often managed to get my children to accomplish more by spinning a story around an adventure in which they were the hero. Dads, your leadership will inspire your kids to discover strengths they didn't know they had.

We once took our young family on an overnight tramp into the Taraweras, a mountain range behind our home in Wellington, New Zealand—very picturesque, but notorious for changeable weather. We tramped in with another family on a beautiful summer afternoon, set up camp, cooked dinner and then settled into our tents for the night. We woke at around 2 am to the sound of pouring rain— our tents were flooded and the river we had crossed that afternoon was now a raging torrent. Several hours later, the Ranger arrived in a Landrover and transported us back across the river, but we still faced a four-hour tramp back, in freezing conditions, with five young children between us.

I decided that this was the time for some psychological warfare. I created a movie adventure story to die for! The heroes were larger than life, had to navigate crocodile-infested waters, carry maidens on their backs, and negotiate obstacles beyond belief and countless in number. In spite of their 'frostbitten' feet and scratched hands, they battled on, because they had hearts as brave as Richard the Lionheart's, and they were as determined as Robert the Bruce! All the children had parts to play. We 'eeked' out the minties and 'scroggin' between scenes! Finally we made it home to hot baths and warm drinks—and the family 'culture' created during that crisis stayed with us.

When I think of maximising opportunities, I am reminded of the story of a man who was having dinner on his own in a restaurant. The waiter approached him and said, 'Sir, there is a lady who needs a table, but we are full tonight. Do you mind if she shares your table?' The man looked up, and the young woman was drop-dead gorgeous. He said, 'No, that's fine.' He began to talk to her and discovered she was from the USA. He asked her if she was a tourist, and she answered that she was working—doing research on which nation had the men with the most sex appeal.
'Oh!' he said. 'So what have you discovered?'
'Well, so far, Native American men appear to have the most sex appeal.'
'So who is rating second?' he asked.
'Scottish men,' she replied, adding, 'By the way, we haven't introduced ourselves. Can I ask your name?'
Capitalising on the moment, he replied, 'Tonto Macpherson!'

The rallying cry for the boys in the movie Dead Poets Society was 'carpe diem'. As a third-form Latin student, I thought that meant 'fish every day!' But I have discovered it means something much more important: 'Seize the day!'

For parents, there really are only a few days to seize. How many years is it from now until your child is eighteen years old? Let's say you have ten years left of parenting a child—plenty of time, you might be thinking. But think back ten years. What were you doing then? It doesn't seem long ago, does it? And I assure you, the next ten years are going to go a lot faster than the last ten. These few short years of your child's childhood go in a flash. Treasure them (and take lots of photos), but don't forget to seize every opportunity and moment they give you to inspire them, keep them safe and develop their talents and their ability to get on with other people. What you are really doing as a parent is helping your children to write their 'life story'.

I believe we can be both a parent and a "hero-friend" to our children. There is nothing mutually exclusive about those terms. But it will be a friendship different from any other your children will have. Your children's other friendships will depend on mutuality. But your kids really want you to be their father, not a favourite easygoing uncle. The best kind of father could be described as the species *parentus backbonicus*. A parentus backbonicus stays on his pedestal: not in an aloof and distant sense, but in the way that a coach does. He's not barking parade-ground orders from a soap box, but he's also not the delinquent father who says, 'Come on kids, let's go and have a beer and a smoke behind the shed, but don't tell your mother.' Parentus backbonicus, or parent-coach, has a heart wrapped in authority—or could it be the other way around?

I believe we should aim to be a dad who has dignity, and who plays by the rules, role-modelling healthy manhood to our children. This is the type of dad children will value as a friend and mentor long after their acne has cleared up.

Being an awesome dad will be your life's finest work.

So Dads, "parent with style" and never stop working on being a hero to your kids.

A STRATEGY FOR GROWING HAPPY CHILDREN

We cannot become individuals unless we have someone who is rationally and irrationally and permanently committed to our welfare and interests. We are nobody without a committed somebody.

Professor Richard Whitfield, Warden, St George's House, Windsor Castle, and Founding Honorary Chairman of the UK National Family Trust

A STRATEGY FOR GROWING HAPPY CHILDREN

✪ Put your arm around each of your children and tell them they're 'awesome'.

✪ Make a life-book for each child—a book that tells his or her own individual life story.

✪ Nurture gratefulness. Have a family rule that says that when someone receives a present, they read the card and thank the person before opening the parcel, or they ring or write to say thank you for the gift before using it or playing with it.

✪ Express your love and commitment to your spouse in front of your children.

✪ Keep your own emotional tank full by enjoying friendship with other men.

✪ Give your children the joy of accomplishment—take time to help each child master skills that develop their natural creativity.

✪ Think up a weekly positive message—such as 'you've got a good mind'—to leave in each child's head.

✪ When you are going on a trip in the car (by yourself), invite one child to accompany you. Talk to your child about your work and ask those 'What do you think?' questions.

C ommitment to our family is the greatest gift that we fathers can give to our children. Our commitment is the undergirding security that will be like a rock on which their future is built.

Children's earliest views of themselves tend to be related to how they see themselves fitting into the big picture and their connection to the significant people around them.

Professor Richard Whitfield, an expert in children's social needs, suggests that, 'Every child subconsciously is needing reassurance about some basic questions. "Do I belong?" "Will I be missed?" "Will there be a promise around me not to feel lonely and wounded?" Most of all, a child's earliest anxieties might be expressed as "I will not know how to behave unless someone shows me, and I will not know how to do things unless someone involves me."'

Every human being needs at least one committed person to "author" them, to help them write their life story. Happy children are those who are secure in their identity in the family because they have that committed person.

You can give your children the gift of a life story when you tell them the folklore of your family. Tell your child her own story. It might start with how you rushed to the hospital the day she was born, and who was there. What Mummy said when she first saw the child, or what Grandad wrote on their first card. Children are likely to ask you to tell them this story again and again, because it is their very own story and it helps them identify their place in the web of loving relationships woven around them.

Record their story in a life book, which might be a combination of a photo album, diary, time-line and scrapbook. In order to crystallise their identity, children love a visual picture of their lives. If you, as a loving adult, walk through a child's life with him, helping to fill in the gaps and interpreting the experiences he has, you will be the best ally your child can have. Let them be involved—by sticking in stickers and special treasures—as you build the book together.

As your children grow, you will be amazed by how often they return to their special life book. When they are not feeling good about themselves for some reason, they often find it comforting to look through their life story and think about when they were little and cute and about the people who were and are their anchors in life. It explains to them where they fit into the family's story. It also gives a powerful message that someone loves them enough to record their life history.

We cannot make our children happy, but we can encourage attitudes that will help them develop happiness as a habit. One child can have a room full of "entertainments" and still be bored: another might have a piece of timber and a few cotton-reels and be completely absorbed for hours.

Imagination, invention and resourcefulness will be a treasure chest that no amount of electronic gizmos and toys can match. From early childhood allow your children to build, create and play act. These activities will be the foundation for all future learning and creativity. If they get stuck with their project, help them get unstuck by suggesting a different way or producing a missing ingredient that will get them going again. If your children build a fort in the back yard, join them for a picnic lunch, and don't forget to pick some flowers for the hostess!

Children are born to learn, and they learn through playing, experimenting, and copying you. Young children are never happier than when you, the big person, are playing with them.

Children need to be given attention and acceptance. Organise a concert for special days such as Christmas afternoon. Let each child prepare an item. Let them have the joy of expectation as they practise and look forward to the event. Organise an audience of yourself and other relatives. Clap, cheer and appreciate their efforts. Your children will gain confidence in this safe, relaxed environment.

My children missed their grandparents terribly when they went away for a trip or a holiday. Grandma always had jugs of coloured water that they were allowed to pour into all sorts of bottles, of different shapes and sizes. They had picnics under the apple tree and went on blackberrying expeditions even on school nights. All simple activities, but the fabric of true happiness.

Our lives are made up of a collage of small memories. Grab

the opportunity for a picnic tea or a game of hide and seek, or the chance to turn a chore into fun with your kids.

Denis Prager, who wrote the book *Happiness is a Serious Problem*, suggests that "gratefulness" is the key to happiness. He says that the less you expect, the more you will be grateful. Help your kids to enjoy the simple and the inexpensive. Children who grow up with very high expectations will often be unhappy, because human nature is insatiable. We are never satisfied with what we have. We have to learn to be happy even though we are not fully satisfied.

Goals and dreams are fine, but high expectations can kill happiness.

If we raise our children as grateful human beings, we will have done wonderfully, especially in this materialistic society.

Comfort, pleasure and good self-esteem are the roots of happiness and contentment. No one can artificially inject these into another human being.

Raising a child on a steady diet of "I am the centre of the universe" is generally quite harmful. Your child is not the centre of the universe and never will be.

Happiness is the basis of how children feel about themselves and how others feel about them. If your children realise that they are good people, and develop self-control so that they can tolerate the frustrating situations that inevitably crop up in life as they grow and mature, you will have done a great job.

A STRATEGY FOR
BUILDING BOYS
INTO MEN

Let's grow boys who give manhood a good name.

A STRATEGY FOR BUILDING BOYS INTO MEN

✪ Being a mentor to your sons will be your life's most important work. Establish communication while your sons are young, and want to be on-board. This will give you a history of communication to plug into as they head into adolescence.

✪ Do things with your sons that give you common interests and opportunities to talk.

✪ Help your sons stay true to their own values and integrity. Give them the tools and the personal skills to remain their own person while maintaining strong and helpful friendships.

✪ Avoid asking 'why?' questions. They will usually get the conversation stuck. Use 'what?' 'how?' 'could?' questions. They work like magic. Commit this list of questions to memory:
'What has to be done?'
'What can I do to help?'
'Could you explain a little more?'
'Could you tell me your reason for asking?'
'What needs to change?'
'What are you trying to accomplish?'

✪ Set high expectations for your boys—believe good, big things of your boys.

We know that boys are not doing well in today's society for a variety of reasons. One is the lack of dads around to teach them how to be men.

The story was told in a wildlife journal about a female elephant and her young bull elephants that had been moved to a new wildlife park. Several juvenile elephants ganged up and attacked a rhinoceros. This is bizarre behaviour for young elephants. Apparently, under normal circumstances, the older bull elephant will teach the young males how to act. In the absence of the adult male, these young juveniles ganged up, creating violence and havoc.

It is not too large a leap to draw some parallels with what happens in human society, when there is a lack of available fathers for young and adolescent boys.

Gender researchers, who have for many years concentrated on girls, are now saying our boys are in trouble and need attention.

Boys start out with several strikes against them. They are more vulnerable physically than girls. More die as babies and they're more often diagnosed with learning disabilities than are girls. In adolescence they're more likely to be suspended from school, commit crimes and attempt suicide (and succeed in committing suicide).

Increasing numbers are becoming perpetrators and victims of violence.

Some experts argue that males fail to fully develop emotionally for several reasons: the way we parent and educate them, the influence of human biology and the influence of popular culture.

The decline of male authority and dominance in our society has devalued traditional male virtues like courage and determination. In addition, we have mixed images of maleness, sometimes confusing strong with violent, virile with promiscuous, adventurous with reckless.

When a father is in the home, there is no doubt that boys have fewer problems. As a father, you can set some standards that your sons can attain.

Teach your son the basics of taking responsibility for himself physically, as well as developing social skills.

This means learning how to eat well, get enough rest and exercise. It also means developing friendship skills, including listening and being able to see another's point of view.

Encourage your son to respect girls and women as equals. Discourage condescending jokes and put-downs. If your son makes a negative comment about women, step in and correct him. Model warm affection and respect for his mother in front of him. If you are no longer with the mother of your son, it is still important to model respect for her.

I can still see, in my mind's eye, my Scottish father, whom I thought was just reading the paper in the next room, suddenly appearing, when he heard me giving my mother a hard time, and saying, 'You'll noo speak to your mother like that!' What my Dad was actually doing, behind the 'front' of the paper was monitoring what was going on in the family.

I suggest that you say something like, 'Hey mate—don't ever speak to your mother like that! I searched the world for her and she is the best thing that ever happened to me. If you give her a hard time—then you will have to answer to me!' Your son's level of respect for his mother will largely stem from the way you respect her, and the reverse is also true for mothers.

HELP YOUR SON LEARN NEGOTIATING SKILLS

Teach him that compromise is a necessary part of human relationships, and is not a sign of weakness or lack of 'backbone'. Let him know that sometimes the manly thing to do is walk away from a fight.

Value your son, not just his accomplishments. At the same time, encourage him to do his best.

Research shows that a child's success is directly related to his/her parents' views of education and their encouragement (or otherwise) of the child. If children are to learn the value of education, they need to see this modelled by their parents and they need to be given evidence that higher education is the doorway to a future.

Recent research which sought to identify what characteristics predicted teenage fatherhood found that the most significant predictor was parental attitude towards education. The second-best predictor—obviously related—was the adolescent's perception of the value of education. Teenagers who don't have clear goals are more likely to engage in risk-taking behaviours with long-term consequences.

Limit the violence your son watches on television, in video games and movies.

Many boys feel compelled to go along with the group, even if the group is involved in destructive behaviour. Competent men have the courage of their convictions and know how to steady themselves against the ebb and flow of the group. Give your sons the lines they need to back out of complicated situations while still keeping face with their peers. For example, when being pressured to drink, your son might say, 'No mate, it's too early for me!'

Practise the questions in the box at the beginning of this chapter: use them often and enjoy watching your son grow into a man.

A STRATEGY FOR ENCOURAGING HELPFULNESS AND CO-OPERATION

Don't drive your kids—inspire them.

A STRATEGY FOR ENCOURAGING HELPFULNESS AND CO-OPERATION

✪ Don't call chores jobs or responsibilities; call them challenges. At certain ages, some chores will be seen as challenges or privileges. For example, a four-year-old will love doing the dishes; a ten-year-old will see cooking the dinner as more of a challenge.

✪ Make work meaningful and fun. Inspire your children to do the job faster or better than last time.

✪ Celebrate a job well done and encourage them to reward themselves—the rule is that you can do what you want to do when you've done what you have to do.

✪ Thank your children when they willingly do a chore or perform a kindness.

It's a tragedy that parents often go to extremes by reacting against the way they were brought up themselves. There are those who drive their children (sometimes driven by their own dreams): 'I never had these opportunities when I was a kid' or, 'I had to work so hard, I want my kids to have better memories'. Then there are the others, who react against the way their fathers drove them and so don't challenge their kids at all, and instead just let them drift.

Inspiring always works better than shaming or nagging. Some say that feedback is the breakfast of champions. It is porbably more accurate to say:

- ✪ Vision is the breakfast.
- ✪ Feedback is the lunch.
- ✪ Self-correction is the dinner.

We all need both vision and feedback. Vision gives direction and destiny and feedback keeps you on track. Your young children will respond to the challenge of how fast they can complete a job, and to rewards and accolades. Children will respond to being asked to do something, with the positive expectation of their co-operation as well as positive feedback.

Rules without reasons tend to create rebellion. We are much more likely to get our children's co-operation if we explain why certain things have to be done and teach our kids to congratulate themselves when they have done a good job. Co-operation is about keeping the team "on-board".

A wise father doesn't just have sporadic fits of fun; he mixes fun in as one of the primary flavours of the home. One of the best things I did with my kids when they were little was create the 'Commando Cleaning Team'. On a Saturday morning I would lead my three kids in an hour's action clean up.

I used to play Colonel Klink from the television programme *Hogan's Heroes*. I would make each child stand by the door of their room after they had finished cleaning-up, and I would do a jackboot march down the hall and say things like, 'Vell you have cleaned your rhooms velly vell! As a reward you vill have the ultimate reward: a change of undervear! Andrew will change with Kim and Kim will change with Jonathan and Jonathan will change with...'

Now that's one of the oldest jokes in the world, but little kids love it. Remember, little children think their father is awesome. Use this belief in your invincibility to inspire them while they are small. You can play any TV or movie character you like, and your kids will love it. They'll be so impressed, they will wonder why Hollywood hasn't discovered you yet! Of course, that awe for your ability does tend to fade: and if you try it with your twelve-year-old, he will probably think you're losing it!

Another fun part of the clean up was the award at the end. When we had finished, I would present the accolades. I would put my open hand up like a trumpet and play a quick trumpet voluntary, then I would say something like, 'Because Jonathan Grant has turned his room from a gorilla's den into a room fit for human inhabitants, I'd like to present him with one chocolate fish!' There were accolades and claps all around as each child had a moment of glory, if only in fun.

Occasionally I would go down to the hot bread shop and buy each child a bun with icing and cream hanging out everywhere as a reward, and they would always have finished their jobs by the time I got back.

Cleaning, in itself, is no one's idea of fun. (If you think it is, you probably need professional help, and you are going to love the years when your kids are teens!) But we had heaps of fun.

Seize the moment... and then tickle it!

William Glasser, the well-known psychologist who introduced 'Reality Therapy', now talks about 'Choice Theory'. He says that we can decide as a family to:

- ✪ choose not to blame,
- ✪ choose not to complain, and
- ✪ choose not to criticise.

He suggests that we can teach our children how to make positive requests of each other and give them problem-solving tools to use instead of blaming and criticising. (See

Family Meetings) Choice Theory means we will not have to revert to blame, criticism or complaining.

Now that is pretty hard for those of us who were brought up defending ourselves and finding someone else to blame, but I assure you, it is possible.

If we set boundaries, then no one can go there, because it is out of bounds. If children aren't allowed to blame, then they have to find other ways of explaining what happened or what they need. We just need to practise these things until they become habits.

The other side of Choice Theory is to learn to choose to compliment and choose to be happy.

One of the challenges for fathers is to teach their children these skills.

'They told us to bring down our own clothes. If we do it, we have clean clothes; if we don't, well we don't. After a day or so of wearing dirty socks, you just do it.' (16-year-old girl)

A STRATEGY FOR HELPING YOUR CHILD BUILD GOOD SELF-ESTEEM

Criticism is easy; achievement is more difficult.

Winston Churchill, House of Commons,
22 January 1941

A Strategy for Helping Your Child Build Good Self-esteem

✪ If you expect the best of your children, they will expect the best of themselves.

✪ Self-esteem will come from inside when your children know that they've made a good choice by themselves, as opposed to carrying out a given instruction.

✪ Offer messages that lock in love, such as:
'You do a great job of thinking for yourself.'
'I bet you feel good when you do such a nice job.'
'You can feel proud of yourself because ...'
'It's OK for you to make mistakes.'
'You don't have to be perfect all the time.'

✪ Let your children know you believe in their ability to solve their own relationship problems, but that you are there if they need you.

✪ Help your children to be their own best friends: best friends accept each other and are always trustworthy.

Self-esteem has become a buzz word in the last few decades, and there is plenty of debate about what high self-esteem for a child represents. Most fathers want their children to feel competent and positive about the world they live in, and to develop their full potential. However, most of us know that we feel best about ourselves when we have accomplished a task, mastered a skill or know that we have acted with integrity.

Foster Cline and Jim Fay, who wrote *Parenting with Love and Logic*, suggest that we actually offer our children a chance to develop that much-needed positive self-concept when we act 'with love enough to allow the children to fail and ... with love enough to allow the consequences of their actions to teach them about responsibility'.

We all know that our children have intrinsic value, but we also know that they can only truly feel good about themselves when they have acted as honourable, generous or responsible people.

They will want to be those sorts of people when we model those values and when we create an atmosphere of acceptance and inspiration. Think how, after the Atlanta Olympic

Games, all the youngsters wanted to be sprinter Michael Johnson, and sprint races were conducted in playgrounds all over the world, whenever there was a group of young boys together. Capitalise on those moments; when your children are young and keen, enrol them in sports teams, music lessons, or help them develop a hobby or interest.

The inspiration that comes from us for our children to be good people will have a lot to do with whether they grow to be good people or not.

Teaching your children self-control and strength of character will help them more than just telling them, 'You're great.' Their first job is to learn the rules, then to follow them and to succeed by them. Then they can have just reason for feeling good about themselves; and they won't resent it, or turn violent, if somebody questions their worth.

When we use praise merely to bolster confidence, instead of encouraging real improvement, praise becomes a devalued commodity. False commendation may do insidious damage. If your children cannot face failure and be taught how to pick themselves up and give it another go, they are unlikely to improve. We can give our children good coaching messages when, for some reason, they have to be "on the bench". Everyone finds themselves "on the bench" sometimes. What matters is what you do to get back into the game, and how you (and your child) play when you do.

A quadriplegic athlete interviewed on television said that he lives with the motto, 'We may all face defeat, but we don't ever have to be defeated.'

An article in the New York Times of May 1998 entitled 'Damn I'm Good' suggests that the self-esteem theories of the 1960s, which contended that low self-esteem was the cause of violence, hate, crime and many other antisocial acts, have basically been discredited. The assumption that children cannot learn or develop properly unless they form a positive self-image has not been backed up by research.

According to this article, subtitled 'An idea whose time has come—and gone?', no study has ever demonstrated a connection between feeling good about oneself and improved performance. Albert Bandura, Professor of Psychology at Stanford University, concludes from his research that 'self-esteem affects neither personal goals nor performance... Some students feel terrible about themselves and become academic and social successes. Others brim with self-confidence, and do awful work.'

Sharon Begley, in an article titled 'When Praise is not OK,' printed in the New Zealand Herald in July 1998, reports how unjustified feelings of self-worth can cause aggression. She discusses the research of two US psychologists—Brad Bushman, of Iowa State University, and Roy Baumeister, of Case-Western Reserve University, Ohio—who examined inflated self-esteem (artificially developed), and found that this sort of unjustified self-esteem, the sort that didn't result from a sense of accomplishment, can trigger hostility and aggression. They found that it had just as powerful an effect on aggression as does the combination of being male, drinking and soaking up media violence. They found that schools often contribute to the problem by viewing self-esteem as the cause of success rather than the result of achievement.

Self-control and genuine accomplishment will make life better for your children, and will make them better citizens.

The quality that makes us humans stand out from animals is our ability to create: to conceptualise a project and then bring it into reality. The joy we get from creating something is huge. Whether it is a painting, a jigsaw, a building project, the satisfaction of achieving a goal is the best builder of self-esteem. This is just as much the case for a young child as it is for an adult.

Alan Loy McInnes, who wrote *Bringing Out the Best in People*, suggests that parents should be like astronomers, who study the stars. We need to look at each child's uniqueness and help him or her become the person that he or she was created to be. If they love collecting insects in bottles, then let that be their "thing" for the time being—take them to museums and get natural history books out of the library. Let them enjoy the feeling of having some specialised knowledge.

For your children, set your expectations higher than you think they can reach—not way higher, just ever so slightly higher. It might be a stretch for them to live up to your expectations, but it will be a healthy and helpful stretch. But also be aware not to maintain the 'stretch' unrelentingly, as unrealistic expectations crush kids, and can shatter self-esteem.

Make sure your children know that you think they are 'good enough': totally accepted and loved.

Remember, children are good observers but poor inter-preters, so your coaching role is going to be necessary to interpret for your child right through childhood. Children are often much harder on themselves than they need to be, and often for the wrong reasons.

There will be times when a bit of coaching is in order. A friend tells how her son came home from school with a self-evaluation form. He had evaluated himself very low on just about everything. She asked him why he had marked himself as 2 out of 10 for appearance. 'Well,' he said, 'I have big ears.' At which she replied that the question was really about the way you look after yourself. 'Do you wash and clean your teeth before you go to school? Do you have a shower each day? Your shoes are always clean, because you clean them every Saturday,' she said. 'Oh,' he said. 'Then I'm probably an 8!'

During adolescence, guiding rather than controlling your children is the key. The central task of adolescents is to develop a sense of self that is separate from the family. So they are busy questioning everything that goes on around them. During this time, teens largely look to their peers for their self-esteem and for approval.

The way your adolescent views himself has a big influence on what sort of friends he chooses, which will in turn influence his behaviour. So concentrating just on his behav-iour and his friends may be looking through the wrong end of the glass; he needs encouragement for his own abilities and interpersonal skills.

Your adolescent will choose a group of friends to match his sense of self-worth. If he doesn't have the confidence to mix with a certain group of peers, his need for self-worth will not allow him to mix with that group. Thus his choice of friends is a consequence of his self-esteem.

If you are worried about your teenager's friends putting pressure on him, try to talk to him in an unthreatening way. Try to connect. 'John, it sounds as if you have a problem with your friend Greg. What are you going to do? Would you like to discuss it?' If John declines your invitation, don't force the issue. If he agrees, then encourage him to find his own solution. He can present his solution to you for your opinion. But don't solve his problem for him. By finding his own solution, he is building self-esteem. He will start to feel proud that he was able to solve the problem himself. If his solution meets with your approval, he will feel good about it, and his self-worth will be positively affected.

A *parentus sergeant majorcus* species of parent would, in this situation, try controlling his son by telling him what to do— forbidding him to mix with those friends, for instance. On the other hand, listening to your son's proposed solutions and offering an opinion based on your experience, is a guiding process. You will be a parentus backbonicus, and will build trust because you leave your teen feeling empowered, able to take control of his own life. He will know that his parents are there when, and if, he should need them.

ENCOURAGE MORE THAN YOU PRAISE

Your adolescent does have good qualities. Look for them. They can be things like any of the following (and lots more besides!):

- ✪   Does he always have a cheerful disposition in the morning?
- ✪   Is he the one who always allows others to be first?
- ✪   Does he discuss interesting topics?
- ✪   Does he tell funny jokes?
- ✪   Does he love reading?

Pick up on these qualities of personality that make your child's character unique and worthy. Comment on them often:

'Sam, We love the way you break the tension with your jokes! Humour is a great asset to have.'

'Andrew, I notice how your friends always seem to off-load on you. You're obviously a good mate. That is a great quality to have in life.'

This sort of communication with your kids encourages them to be proud of their good qualities. This builds self-esteem. They come to like themselves, and, more importantly, to know what their strengths are. They will then begin to use these strengths with confidence as they interact with others.

Children with healthy self-esteem always know their strengths and weaknesses. Teach them their strengths; I'll bet they already know pretty well what their weaknesses are!

A STRATEGY FOR
TUNING OUT WORK AND
TUNING INTO HOME

I'm thankful for my family. Sure they've stomped on my ego, invaded my privacy and exposed me at my worst. But if it weren't for them, I might've forgotten what fun feels like. I might've been too embarrassed to make sandcastles on the beach, play hide and seek in the backyard, or chuck waterbombs around the kitchen.

John Cooney, Editor, Grapevine Magazine

A STRATEGY FOR TUNING OUT WORK AND TUNING INTO HOME

✪ As you drive home, choose a landmark which will be your cue to stop thinking about work and start thinking about home. Think about your arrival and the children who are dying to see you.

✪ If it is safe, suggest to your wife that she send the children to the end of the street to wait for you (just to the letterbox will do), then you pick them up and deliver them home.

✪ Play their favourite music on your cassette as they jump into the car.

✪ Let each of them carry something inside for you.

✪ Make an entrance each night! Open the door and ask 'Where is the most awesome woman in the world?' 'Where are the greatest kids in the world?' Or something similar—whatever is right for you!

✪ Play a game each night with your children for ten minutes—it may be the same game every night, until they get tired of it. Then set a boundary on your own need for space. Tell them that now it is your time to sit and talk to Mummy.

It has been said that one of a working man's greatest needs is for tranquillity at home. How can we mix this need with the expectation of our families for our attention when we arrive home after a busy day? And of course most mothers would like a bit of tranquillity in the home, too! After all, whether they are out in the workforce or are full-time on the domestic front, they are tired in the evening, too.

I suggest that you concentrate on a plan to give your children and wife or partner some positive attention first and then set some boundaries on your own need for space.

Mary used to complain that the dog got the first welcome, the children the second, and she was the last in line for the hug and the kiss.

Model commitment for your wife. Seek her out first. This will be the best thing you can do for your children—love their mother and show it!

Follow this up by a big welcome for your children. 'Where are the greatest kids in the world?' or something similar.

Give your children fifteen minutes attention when you come in the door. Play a game, hear their news or have races up the hallway!

Try to discipline yourself to smile and think about the value of that ten minutes fun time.

Bring home surprises.

A STRATEGY FOR
AFFIRMING YOUR
CHILD

*Affirming words from parents are like light switches—speak
a word of affirmation at the right moment and it is like
lighting up a room full of possibilities.*

John Trent, 'Leaving the Light On'

A STRATEGY FOR
AFFIRMING YOUR CHILD

✪ Positively label your children whenever possible so that they see themselves as helpful, honest, reliable or loving people. The labels people around us give us tend to stick!

✪ When praising your child, make sure you know what the underlying message behind your praise is.

✪ Make sure you are reinforcing something your child can actually do something about.
Don't just say: 'You look nice.'
Say: 'I like the way you dressed yourself and brushed your hair.'

✪ Make sure that if you affirm (or console) a child who comes home from school with poor marks on a report, you are not sending the child the message that poor marks are OK, and that you really don't expect any more from the child. Acknowledge that you are disappointed, and affirm that you know the child can do better and that you expect him or her to try harder next time.

✪ Only measure their improvement against themselves (not against their friends or siblings), and be sure to praise and affirm their improvements.

Cultivate the habit of complimenting both your spouse and your children. When our children are little we tend to praise them to bits. They are cute and they think that we are invincible.

All children need to hear 'Well done, you did a great job.' Especially as they grow up.

I will never forget the afternoon I took my family to see the Russian circus, a novelty that rarely came to our city. Our four-year-old son was sitting between my legs, with eyes as wide as saucers. When a trapeze artist made a huge swan dive followed by two double flips, to the loud clanging of cymbals and dramatic musical climax. I said to him, 'Wow Johnny, what did you think of that?' To which he replied, 'Oh you could do that Dad, no sweat!' I lived on that for weeks!

But the point must be made that it is very easy to affirm a little fellow who thinks that you can "walk on water"; it is harder to give affirmation to those whose actions are unloveable and ugly. Our children's obnoxious and unloveable behaviour may have something to do with how they are feeling about themselves; it has been said that children and teenagers are most obnoxious when they most need love.

Teenagers probably need compliments more than anyone. They are negotiating identity crises in a very real sense.

At about age fourteen they will be pushing you away, trying to get their head around who they are and whether they like what you stand for. Your unthreatened and unthreatening responses will be a gift as they struggle towards the independence and responsibilities of adulthood. Affirm your belief in their character, and in their ability to make good decisions, and make sure you affirm their good judgement by giving them reasons for the boundaries you set for them.

Silence is not always golden; our children need to hear us affirm their worth and acceptance out loud.

Positively labelling our children is a powerful mechanism for moulding their view of themselves. A friend tells how during her student years, when self-doubt threatened to trip her up at exam time, she would hear her father's voice in her head saying, 'You've got a good mind.' His words were enough to help her redouble her efforts.

The most influential modifier of children's behaviour is their parents' expectations. When we parents expect the best of our children, and communicate that expectation to them, they will be more likely to operate out of that trust and belief that we have in them.

Many experts are concerned about the rising levels of co-dependent people in our society. By controlling others, co-dependent people discover that they can establish some semblance of control over their own lives. According to Dr Frank Minirth and Dr Paul Meier, of the Minirth-Meier Clinic in USA, co-dependency can be an addiction to people, behaviours, or things, as someone tries to control his internal feelings by controlling people, things, or external events (Robert Hemfelt, Frank Minirth and Paul Meier, *Love Is a Choice*, Thomas Nelson 1989).

In many cases, a person's co-dependency can be traced to a childhood that left a huge gap in his or her life – where parents were not available to meet childhood needs. Many people trapped by drugs and alcohol or other addictions, are haunted by voices from their childhood saying things like 'Try harder. You never do anything right.'

Give your children better messages than these.

Affirm their value to you, their ability to think for themselves and their honesty and courage. Teach them that the future is their friend and that they can reward themselves with internal messages about a job well done: 'You handled that well.' Teach them the significance of a kind act or word.

At a recent Father's Breakfast at which I was a speaker, one of the other participants was an ex-prisoner who had led riots in a Brisbane prison several years previously. He spoke about his childhood, and how his angry, dismissive and blaming father constantly put him down both in private and in public. He explained how as a small boy, he would wet his pants trying not to do the wrong thing around his father. However, in his nervousness, he ended up doing silly things, and so incurred more ridicule and anger. Later on, as a teenager, he ran away from home and lived on the streets. He said that all the street kids he mixed with in those years had fathers like his.

Beware, fathers: if you don't like your children (or if you fail to communicate adequately to them that you do like them), your children will not like themselves.

People become what we encourage them to be, not what we nag them to be. When a child is acting badly, try saying 'This isn't like you!' Help the child understand the kind of behaviour that you want to affirm—expect that behaviour, and label your child's character as better than the current behaviour.

Try catching your child doing something good and praise him!

Praise your small children when they are playing nicely. Don't wait until a fight develops or they begin whining and complaining. Make sure they get attention when they are being co-operative and good, not just when they are behaving badly.

Unfortunately, children will settle for bad attention rather than no attention at all. Don't wait until they are all fighting for what seat they will sit on in the car. Give a different child the leadership each day, in rotation, and affirm each one's ability to be fair in allocating seats for his siblings.

Tell another adult, within earshot of the child, something that you appreciate about that child.

I have a good friend who is a very successful entrepreneur. He has concluded that people who do well in the business world have an ability to affirm the people around them. He decided that it was a habit that he would encourage in his family. So each Friday night, they have a family tradition of distributing 'Honk' cards. Each Friday night he gives each family member honk cards to write encouraging messages for every other family member. The Honk cards have a picture of geese who, as they fly long distances to migrate, take turns at taking the lead. They apparently honk to encourage each other on. (Saatchi and Saatchi produced community-service television advertisements using this concept.) My friend was amused to discover his eight-year-old son had written to his sister, 'I think that you are a very good dancer, you have feet like a dog's feet!' No doubt, to this eight-year-old, having dog's feet was the ultimate compliment!

Positive words are important, because they fill up our emotional tank. When we have a healthy bank balance, we hardly notice a few withdrawals, but if the account is running low, those few withdrawals become extremely significant! The same applies with our emotional tank.

Children living on a low emotional tank are really battered by setbacks, small criticisms and even mild discipline, whereas a child who has had positive attention (and therefore has a full tank) is much more resilient.

Fathers need to be aware that blame and shame are not the way to motivate children. Not only because they don't work, but also because blaming, criticising and complaining eat away at identity like corrosive acid. They put us all on the defensive and stop us all from growing.

Why did Jesus say that words kill? (In fact, he used some of his strongest words to warn people not to call others idiots or to curse them.) Because those words tend to become a tape in your children's heads, and will be constantly replayed. They can also create a ceiling on how they view their ability and worth.

Be firm and kind. Recognise that, as important as protecting your child's physical safety is, protecting their sense of self and their feeling of their own value in the family and the world, is equally vital.

A horse's confidence is vital in a race. If he is happy in his position, he will perform well. Humans are the same—when we are confident, we perform.
Darren Beadman—Dual Melbourne-Cup-Winning Jockey

A STRATEGY FOR
A GREAT
FATHERS' DAY

Don't wait. Do it now. See your family now. Take the trips now. Speak your love to them today and every day. Take advantage of the time. Tomorrow may never come.

Bob Overton, 'Faces of Fatherhood'

A STRATEGY FOR A GREAT FATHERS' DAY

✪ Tell your children that you are so proud to be their father, and that to celebrate Fathers' Day you are going to throw a party that will include taking them on a mystery trail. You can do this with a voucher system, or a set of clues, or you could let each child choose one thing he or she would like to do. Perhaps:

a game of mini golf,

or a ride in a train or cable car or ferry,

or lunch at a fast food store,

or rollerblading,

or a game of cricket.

✪ Make sure that each activity takes only about half an hour, so boredom doesn't set in and you can maintain a sense of momentum about the day.

✪ Try any of the other ideas in this chapter.

I n many households, Fathers' Day is a hassle. Mothers rush round the day before trying to think of something that you would like, and it ends up being sort of a repeat birthday, with all sorts of expectations that put pressure on a busy family.

RE-CAPTURE FATHERS' DAY!

Take the initiative in having fun with your family. You could, of course, just settle for a boring old traditional Fathers' Day: a card, breakfast in bed—that is, providing it gets as far as your bedroom; mine usually ended up being spilled halfway down the passage!—the useful-but-pretty-predictable socks, and a tie you could never wear in public unless you'd had a taste-bypass operation. Or you could change all that.

Why not start with: 'This Father's Day I want to celebrate the fact that I have the privilege of being the coach of this awesome team.'

Then plan an incredible day—or afternoon—and I don't just mean taking the children to McDonald's. Do you want your kids to remember you as a boring old drongo, sitting at a fast food establishment, reading the paper while the kids play? Plan the time so that every half-hour you're doing something new and exciting. Make sure it's exciting for the kids and not just for you.

Take the initiative and "Go for Gold" with your kids on Fathers' Day!

You set the agenda! Tell them that you are expecting home-made cards from them. Tell them you're not going to settle for these bought ones with a second-hand message on them; you really prefer the cards that they make themselves and the messages that they write themselves!

Then tell them that they are 'allowed' to give you breakfast in bed—that's their privilege. Your privilege is to be their father, and you would like to celebrate Fathers' Day by making it a "Dad's Big Day Out". It's party time!

Treat it a bit like Christmas Eve—they all have to get a good night's sleep the night before the big day, so it's early to bed for them all. This is one way to raise the expectation level a few notches.

After your breakfast in bed and the ritual card reading, give them a specific time to report to the kitchen, dressed and ready to go on your Fathers' Day excursion. They will all have to have their beds made and chores done, so you will also need to orchestrate a bedroom inspection at a certain time. Make it fun too!

Make a ritual of checking that they have everything they will need for the day—you could post a list of things they need to bring with them on the fridge, perhaps.

Make each of them a team leader for a certain activity, but keep the power of veto yourself, so that you can take over as team leader if you wish, at any time.

Remember, in your busyness, you may have recently come across to your children as Dad the Policeman, or Dad the Comatose TV Watcher. So this is your chance to set the record straight and be Dad the Adventurer. Unfortunately, although we would like to think of spontaneous fun just happening, if you don't plan it, it usually won't happen.

Find out what is 'hot' with the kids right now, and try to build in an activity for each child. If you have a six-year-old who is into animals in a big way, perhaps you could build in a visit to a pet shop.

Try to finish the day on a high.

Try a wild water balloon fight (but make sure you have their mother on your side for this!). Or:

✪ Fill a hundred or so balloons with water and tie the ends.
✪ Form a giant circle with the garden hose.
✪ Give each child about twenty balloons.
✪ Stand in the centre of the circle.

The rules are that:

✪ Only one child can throw a balloon at a time.
✪ As soon as a balloon breaks, somebody else can throw theirs.
✪ Whoever 'hits' Dad gets 10 cents.

- ✪ When Dad catches a balloon, fires it back and 'hits' a child, he gets 5 cents from that child.

This game will be sheer unforgettable pandemonium!

Don't forget the hot chocolate and the warm baths afterwards.

Remember, someone who is a hero to his kids is someone who spends time with them, models playing fair, protects them, and has fun.

Here are some other ideas:

- ✪ Slide down a hill on plastic bags.
- ✪ Go on a dinosaur hunt.
- ✪ Wrap your in-laws' car in toilet paper.
- ✪ Catch a ferry.
- ✪ Go busking.
- ✪ Hire tandem bikes.
- ✪ Picnic in the park or at the beach.
- ✪ Make a funny video.
- ✪ Fly kites.
- ✪ Get photographed by Japanese tourists.
- ✪ Have an indoor picnic, complete with swimsuits and towels.
- ✪ Play board games in a shopping mall.
- ✪ Dress as tourists and do fake greetings and goodbyes at the airport.
- ✪ Have a tramp's picnic under a bridge (watch out for real tramps!).
- ✪ Take a 'coin-flip' drive—at each intersection, flip a coin: heads, turn left, tails, turn right.

Of course, finish with a takeaway meal—it is Fathers' Day, after all.

I tell you, your kids will never forget Fathers' Day if you take this kind of creative initiative.

The trouble will be, of course, maintaining the standard for next year!

A Strategy for Developing Your Child's Character

Human beings must be trained in obedience to moral intuitions almost before they are rational enough to discuss them, or they will be corrupted before the time for discussion arrives.

C.S. Lewis

It is easier to build boys than to fix men.

Author unknown

A STRATEGY FOR DEVELOPING YOUR CHILD'S CHARACTER

✪ If you expect the best of your children, they will rise to your expectations.

✪ Label your children positively—trustworthy, honest, loveable, kind—and you will find that they will grow into the labels you give them.

✪ Remember your three allies—influence, information and internalisation.

✪ Teach your children the values you want them to live by.

✪ Turn the television off and read to your children. Stories of heroes and heroines are ideal. Read to them at bedtime, and at mealtimes. Read them the great classics that teach honour and courage, love and sacrifice.

✪ Walking, whether it's around the corner to the video shop, along the beach or tramping through the hills, is a good time for talking to your children.

✪ Teach your children the family sayings that have been passed on from your parents:
'Honesty is the best policy.'
'A good name is better than riches.'

✪ When your child steps over a boundary that involves a family value, deal with it. Help your child put it right and feel the relief of a clear conscience.

One of our greatest privileges, as well as one of our greatest responsibilities, is to hand on wisdom to the next generation. One of the characteristics that sets humans apart from animals is the fact that animals are born with instinct, whereas humans learn almost everything from their parents.

I recently heard Dr Bruce Perry, an expert on children's brain development, speak about the importance of consistent parenting in the early years of a child's life. He suggested that if we don't take our role of nurturing our children seriously, we can lose the 'cultural DNA' of families within a generation. In other words, our children won't have the 'wiring' to know how to nurture their children if they don't experience that nurturing from us.

I would suggest that it is equally important for us to hand on a culture of family values to live by. The training and boundaries that you give your children will be your grandchildren's inheritance.

It has been said that children's habits determine their character, and their character determines their future.

Traditionally, family wisdom and oral history were handed down around the campfire or the meal table, and parents took it for granted that it was their role to coach and train their children, and develop their character. However, these days, with busy lifestyles and both parents working, it is all too easy to lock into survival mode, and put "on hold" the meal-time discussions and character training, and hope that the teacher or the babysitter or the child care worker is doing it.

However, this training is our role, and it can be a hugely rewarding one, especially if the atmosphere in which we teach is safe and the teaching can be turned at least partly into fun.

Unfortunately, children don't come already trained, and whether we like it or not, they will sometimes develop habits and attitudes which we need to train them out of!

We will have to give attention and encouragement to replacing those negative attitudes with positive ones.

This could actually be seen as a self-serving exercise because there is a good chance that if we take the time to do this while our children are young, we are likely to become freer from parental responsibilities as the years go by, because we have inspired our kids to become self-directed, trustworthy human beings.

Recent research indicates that one of the best ways to develop character in our children is to read them stories that involve role models—heroes and heroines from all walks of life, from today or from the past, real people or the stuff of fiction, Bible stories, fairytales or Classical myths and legends.

Reading to children is providing them with some of the best special attention you can give them. It is an opportunity for closeness, discussion and the ideas that program the hard drive in our kids' heads.

When they are little, you can sit them on your knee or cuddle up in front of the fire and read or tell them their favourite stories—over and over again if necessary! I used to add bits into the story and suddenly the children would find that they were the characters in a C.S. Lewis novel or a fairytale. Even the family dog made it into a few! And they were always on the alert for an inauthentic bit or any missed pages! As you ask your children questions about the story and let them pretend to read it themselves, you will form a strong and unique bond.

Later, as your children grow older, take turns to read at the dinner table. Maybe once a week read a short article or a story. Ask questions at the end, so that you can "jumpstart" a family discussion and keep in touch with your children's developing consciences and values.

Children learn about character by hearing stories with morals. In the progression of the story, they see the outcomes of good and bad choices. As they identify with the heroes and heroines in the story, they will experience vicariously the impact of the decisions and behaviour of those heroes and heroines. Read your children the classics, books that teach universal principles such as:

- ✪ you will reap what you sow, and
- ✪ the value of truthfulness and selflessness.

William Bennett's *Book of Virtues* is a bestseller. It is an anthology of classic morality tales that will give your kids a great heritage.

We must also decide which values we ourselves believe in and live by. We need to let our children know that we live by an ethic. The Judaeo-Christian ethic, based on the Ten Commandments and the Sermon on the Mount, has been the foundation of much of Western society. It is interesting to note that when Moses was given the Commandments, God instructed him to tell the fathers to teach them to their children at mealtimes, at bedtime and when they were out walking. These are the relaxed times, when your children are likely to be enjoying your presence and open to your fatherly wisdom.

Many traditional cultures, including Maori, Samoan and Australian Aboriginal, have a rich tradition of storytelling, which communicates their heritage – where they come from and where they are going – and moral base, and grants them a strong sense of attachment.

In our role as family coaches, we have three 'in's as allies. They are:

- ✪ influence,
- ✪ information, and
- ✪ internalisation.

We have the influence of our example and teaching. We can

teach right and wrong, not just because it generates the best long-term results (which it does), but because it is the right thing to do.

We can give our children information. Most parents manage to communicate their rules, but they often fail to give the reasons behind them. A recent US survey of 11 to 18-year-olds showed that when children had a firm basis for their values, it made a big difference to all sorts of behaviour. The survey showed that when young people lacked an objective standard of truth (the logic of the family rules), they became three times more likely to cheat in an exam, twice as likely to steal, three times more likely to use illegal drugs, twice as likely to be angry with life and six times more likely to attempt suicide.

We can also help our youngsters internalise values. We will not always be there to make sure that they 'toe the line'. Internal control is vital if your children are to develop real character; the 'rules' need to be taken from the head and written on the heart. Gently training a child's conscience—helping the child recognise the feeling that making a good choice gives—will help fertilise the child's sense of responsibility for his or her own life.

Our children won't remember much of what we tell them if we are stern and preachy, but they will remember the feeling of a clear conscience when we helped them tell the truth and stood behind them as they faced up to a wrong action, helping them to put a situation right.

They are most likely to internalise the information we give them, and to respond to the influence that we try to have on them, if the atmosphere is warm and loving but also consistent.

Our elder son tells the story of a childhood event which is still indelibly imprinted on his psyche. Their mother was driving them home after a visit to relatives, and he and his siblings were talking in the back seat about how their young cousin had cried because they had ganged up on her. He recalls that he heard his mother's voice from the driver's seat, asking firmly, 'And were you mean to your cousin?' On confessing he says that he and the other backseat mini-gangsters were startled as their mother whirled the car in a high-speed U-turn and drove straight back to their cousin's house. He was given the task of apologising, and admitting that he hadn't thought about what it would be like for his cousin, being treated like that. He has never forgotten this lesson, which he learned at the age of six!

Barbara Coleroso, who has written some superb parenting books including *Kids Are Worth It*, suggests that it is vital for us to give our children these three things: ownership of their own problems, the tools to solve them and their dignity intact.

I believe that a clear conscience is something that we can help our children learn to identify. If they have done something morally wrong—lying, stealing or hurting someone—they need to know how to say sorry, and they need to put things right with the other person. If they have broken something or messed up, they need to be able to fix it. A good plan is to have a list of special jobs for when children have broken a family rule. They can apologise, but by way of restitution, they must choose one of the jobs on the list.

It may be sweeping the drive, bringing in firewood, or something similar. I believe that the dynamic that is in operation here would help the rehabilitation of many prisoners—everyone needs the opportunity to take responsibility for their actions, to connect with the fact that what they did has affected others and do something to put things right.

The information we give our children will be the stuff out of which they create their own set of values. We can to teach them why doing the right thing has advantages, by showing them the natural, logical consequences of their actions. They need to know that if they do the right thing, they will not ever have to live with the long-term consequences of being labelled a cheat, or a thief, for instance; they will have a good reputation. But we also need to teach them that altruism (doing the right thing because it is the right thing to do) is the best way to live because there is an external set of moral values that underpins the universe, and by keeping a clear conscience one can also sleep at night.

The Family Virtues Guide, by Linda Kavelin Popov with Dan Popov and John Kavelin, and Teaching Your Children Values, by Linda and Richard Eyre, are both books which list the virtues identified by C.S. Lewis in Illustrations of the Tao, as being central to over twenty major civilisations (from Australian Aboriginal to Hindu). They are:

- ✪ honesty and truthfulness,
- ✪ kindness,
- ✪ consideration and concern for others,
- ✪ compassion,

- ✪ obedience,
- ✪ responsibility,
- ✪ respect, and
- ✪ duty.

These universal virtues are common to all peoples at all times, and are an objective guide to decent human behaviour.

A journalist, in a magazine article, described this photograph. It was of a man dressed in black, wearing a distinctive a black hat with curls coming down the side of his head. He is a Hasidic Jew. The father is bending down talking to his son, who is dressed the same way. The boy is looking up into his father's face with a look of complete trust. As you pull back in the photo, you see there is a soldier in uniform with a rifle pointed at the father's head. Surrounding the three figures are hundreds of dead bodies. The photo is from the Holocaust. The journalist guesses that the shutter of the camera and the trigger of the rifle were pulled at the same time.

The question the journalist poses is: 'How is it that this young boy, in such a moment of terror, can look so trustingly into his father's face?'

Could it be that the Jewish father had been telling the great stories of Old Testament heroes to his son from when the boy was tiny? That he had given his son the building blocks of character by helping him identify with courageous figures in true stories? It would appear that he had also built trust. I wonder if the boy was thinking, 'I'm scared stiff, but I can trust Dad—he knows what to do.'

I want to be a father like the one in that picture.

Help your children take responsibility for their attitudes and behaviour.

Your daughters will be the nurturers of the future generation. Their strong character, combined with women's natural ability to help people work together, will be their contribution to a better world. Your contribution is to help them achieve this.

Don't encourage a "boys will be boys" attitude in your sons, that excuses selfishness and domination. If your son hurts someone, ensure that he apologises. Teach him that mature masculinity is about having principles. Show him, by your example, how to act in an ethical and compassionate way.

Help all your children understand that we live in communities and that individual wants can't be pursued at the expense of the good of the group (or the relationship), be it the family, the neighbours, or the workforce.

If you want to help your children see the consequences of doing the right thing—of telling the truth, not stealing, not cheating, for instance—you might like to try the chart on the next page. I use it in high schools and clubs (but it can be quite well understood by children from age eight or nine).

Draw up a chart then get the children to think up advantages and disadvantages of right and wrong behaviour and fill in the blanks. You will find as you fill in the chart that:

- ✪ the disadvantages of doing right are short term and the disadvantages of doing wrong are long term, and
- ✪ the advantages of doing right are long term and the disadvantages of doing right are short term.

The logic of choosing to live honest lives may click for your children.

	ADVANTAGES	DISADVANTAGES
RIGHT	(LONG TERM)	(SHORT TERM)
WRONG	(SHORT TERM)	(LONG TERM)

When children make mistakes or break rules, don't think of it as a problem—but as a significant learning opportunity. Remember it's not what your children do that is important; it is how you handle the situations when they arise.

A STRATEGY FOR
STEALING TIME FOR
YOUR KIDS

Time is a circus, always packing up and moving away.

Ben Hecht

A STRATEGY FOR STEALING TIME FOR YOUR KIDS

❊ Write your family times in your diary.

❊ Take a child with you in the car whenever possible, and talk with the child.

❊ Avoid night meetings, or at least plan to be home three nights a week.

❊ Tell your kids an ongoing story that involves your child (or children). You can do this while shaving or at bedtime.

❊ Roster yourself with your child to do chores.

❊ Try to schedule time with your teenager, perhaps to play a game of golf or go to a football game together or a good movie. There may be some 'white water' (rough) times during these years, but try to keep your eyes open for your teenager's interests and stretch a little for the sake of the relationship.

❊ Have a sport or hobby you share with your pre-teenager.

❊ Give your kids their own toolboxes and some of your real tools. (This also gives you a great excuse to buy some new ones!)

❊ Avoid committees like the plague, or ask (about every meeting), 'Is this meeting really important?'

Remember kids spell love T.I.M.E.

You may think 'I'll give my kids all the time that's left over after I have done the important stuff', but you will find that your leftover time will get squeezed, and will become shorter and shorter. Your kids are the important stuff. They deserve better than leftovers.

You need to actually block out time in your diary.

You need to get an answering machine and use it, especially at mealtimes and story times. Let's face it: we will probably only ever get about five desperately urgent phone calls in our whole lifetime. The rest can happily compost in our voice mail. Try videoing the evening news and watch it after dinner. Make mealtimes fun, communicating times.

A Strategy for Communicating with Your Children

Children who do not take part in healthy family rituals will often go looking for them in the form of the violence offered by gangs.

Paul Pearsall, 'The Power of the Family for Strength, Comfort and Healing'

If men ruled the world, nodding and looking at your watch would be deemed an acceptable response to "I love you".

Author Unknown

A STRATEGY FOR COMMUNICATING WITH YOUR CHILDREN

Establishing family 'traditions' will help keep the lines of communication open.

✪ Phone your children from work and ask how their day has been.

✪ Stay in touch with your children when they are away from home.

✪ Take the initiative to make contact with your family— don't always leave it to your wife or partner.

✪ Write your children a special Dad's Letter every year telling them how proud of them you are.

✪ Make the time to listen to them when they want to talk. Of course they need to learn about 'can it wait?' or 'not now, Dad's busy'. But if Dad's always busy, remember that he will be losing a lot of opportunities!

✪ Apologise. If we say 'sorry' to our children when we blow it or disappoint them, they are learning good behaviour from us. The world is yet to see the perfect parent, so we are all going to fail sometimes! Saying sorry is the quickest way to get the relationship back on track.

They don't care that you know, until they know that you care.

Family traditions are a powerful medium for keeping family communication flowing. Those cultures with strong family traditions provide children with a web of security, as well as many occasions for connection between parents and their kids.

Psychologists tell us that if you grow up in a family with strong rituals, you're more likely to be resilient as an adult.

Rituals are a stabilising force in children's lives, because they give our kids the predictability they need and they open up natural, informal discussion between family members. For children to know that 'we always do this' is very healthy. The daily, weekly and yearly traditions that you, as a dad, establish will be the memories that your children treasure. The yearly 'Fathers' Day', the weekly family meeting, the nightly chat on the end of their bed; these are your lifelines for staying in touch with your kids.

Establishing rituals in the family can be your chance to use innovation and creativity. Whether you come from a family that had strong traditions or not, work out with your wife or partner which traditions from the past you will carry on and what new ones you will create. Whether it is the way you announce your arrival home every night, or what your family does for dinner on a Friday, or how you celebrate Christmas Eve, these special times will be anchors that your children refer back to.

I remember my own Grandad disappearing every Christmas Day just before Father Christmas arrived. My sister and I were distraught that 'Da', as we called him, always went for his afternoon swim just at that time and always missed Father Christmas's visit! However, when my children were small, the same Father Christmas suit was recycled for my Dad, who managed to convince our small fry that he had urgent business, also just before Father Christmas arrived at the family 'do'!

But the tradition that our children seemed to love most was Christmas Eve around the tree. Mary would prepare Christmas fruit mince pies, and I would serve sparkling grape juice, in the best champagne glasses. We would turn off the lights, and by candlelight would sing carols and read the Christmas story. We would then share the year's best blessing, the year's best book, the year's best news, and so on, and finish with a family prayer. When our children were small, they would often ask if their friends could stay for Christmas Eve, because 'they don't have the family reading and talk at their place!' You might like to let your children open one present at that stage—or you could think up some other little ritual.

When our children began bringing home their future

spouses, we continued the tradition, but on the first year, after reading the Christmas story, we decided to get each person to briefly tell their 'life story'. It was a moving time, and we learned a great deal about the lives of the young women who turned out to be our daughters-in-law. As they talked about their lives and the experiences that had shaped them, we gained an understanding of who they were as people which created a special sense of closeness for us as a family.

We all need some constants that we can count on in our lives. It has been said that rituals are the mortar that help hold families together when a crisis comes.

Birthday rituals and family meals are valuable for your child's sense of identity.

In our family we always had a second birthday party for each child the day after the party for their friends. This was just a family dinner, but the ritual associated with this dinner was that each member of the family had to give a speech to the person whose birthday it was. The rule was that it had to be a positive speech, saying only the things that you liked and valued about this family member.

There were many spin-offs from this family tradition. Our children learned to speak publicly, practising in a safe situation; they each heard the rest of the family say what they admired and respected about them; and my sons learned to mock their Dad in a positive way! When it came to the speeches about me on my birthday, the 'positive and affirming bit' was sometimes fairly deeply buried under plenty of good-humoured ribbing. My daughter was always very sweet (and still is), but my sons learned how to mock me—especially my enthusiasm for gadgets and power tools—eloquently (in a 'positive and affirming' way, of course!).

Our children now bring their in-laws home for this birthday ritual and it is quite common for the speeches to go on and on! The family retell stories from their childhood; stories which often become exaggerated with the telling, and we find ourselves laughing and reliving the events as we enjoy the shared history!

So instigate the family birthday party, and give a great speech that sets the tone.

Play Mighty Memories after an anniversary or Christmas dinner. Encourage everyone to share his or her favourite childhood memory. You will learn things about your children that you won't hear any other way!

Take your child to work with you for a day.

Listen to tapes and ask what the child thinks about the subject or the song. Then ask her how she came to that conclusion. Take the opportunity to ask your child's opinion.

Take your children to help you buy a shirt or tie. It can be a lot of fun and you may even end up better dressed!

Take your children along when you are going to a sports shop, or doing something that will need some "muscle power", like picking up some timber or bricks. Even a small child will feel important if he helps stack a huge pile of firewood.

A good friend tells of the day that he helped his father lay a concrete drive. At the age of eight, he was honoured to be his father's right-hand man. But the best part was the fact that his dad kept his promise—he took him to the movies that night and taught him how to throw popcorn in the air and catch it in his mouth. Thinking back, he says his father was probably exhausted, but keeping his promise to his son left a great memory.

When we keep our promises to our kids, even when it hurts, it says 'you are important to me', loud and clear.

Fathers can save themselves and their kids a lot of grief if they can instil the 3 R's in them. Not readin', writin' and 'rithmetic, but:

- ✪ respect,
- ✪ responsibility, and
- ✪ resourcefulness.

RESPECT

According to police, one of the biggest problems amongst young people today is that they lack respect for themselves and others. Respect comes from the amount of value you attach to things. How can you get your children to readjust their valuation of themselves and others? You get this 'R' from this 'aaaahhh!' 'Aaaahhh' is a noise that comes from somewhere deep in your chest and indicates delight and enthusiasm about whatever your eye has just fallen on. An 'Aaaahhh' as your son walks into the room is very different from a groan, a sigh or a muttered obscenity. As well as 'Aaaahhh', try stirring in:

'How's my best mate?'

'Where's the most awesome daughter in the world?'

When you arrive home, make sure your entrance communicates 'Aaaahhh'. Call your daughters gorgeous, talented, awesome. Call your sons handsome, great, tough.

Developing respect involves showing respect, and valuing your children's opinions does this. Invite their ideas, and listen to them.

Your children will learn to respect themselves as they see you respect them. But they must also learn that your respect can be lost. Your disappointment in their moral failures throws your pleasure in their success and triumphs into sharp relief.

RESPONSIBILITY

Your children have to become (and trust themselves to be) responsible for their own actions. Every action has consequences, and their choices and decisions will set in train events that they must face up to. Young people live within a tiny slice of time; the perspective that we have as adults, our ability to see the long-term results of some actions, must be lent to our kids.

Never rescue your kids from the consequences of their actions—you would be robbing them of their most valuable educational opportunities. When they blow it, say, 'That's sad. How are you going to solve it?' Part of teaching responsibility is teaching problem-solving.

RESOURCEFULNESS

You can never make your teenager happy. But you can give

your children the gift of contentment and the ability to create, so that they can make themselves happy. From early childhood, we need to make sure there is a space in the house or garage where they can build, create and make a mess.

A hunger for information and the ability to get it are great resources. Introduce your kids to libraries. Of course, they'll take to the Internet even quicker and more naturally than you do.

Let every child do what he can for himself. It is excruciating to see a child make mistakes, but it's exhilarating to see your child succeed. Don't rush to give children all the answers. Instead, teach them to tell themselves the truth and learn effective problem-solving techniques.

PROBLEM SOLVING

Stop! If your child is stuck on something and frustrated, don't step in and fix it. Ask 'what is the problem?' Interrupt impulsive reactions whenever possible, and help your child calm down. Then help him think through the problem to the solution. Identify the problem by asking questions until you understand exactly what your child is saying to himself. Is it true?

THINK!

What can be done about the problem? Have your child think (and maybe talk) about all the possible solutions. Write them down if that is feasible, and would help your child.

CHOOSE!

Help your child consider the likely consequences of each

solution and select the one with the best outcome. Put a tick next to the best one if the options have been written down.

ACT!

Try the solution. Review it. Did it work? If it did, the problem is solved. If it didn't, try another solution from **Think!**

Then repeat **Choose!** and **Act!**

Again, it is important your children know that if it matters to them, it matters to you.

This doesn't mean that you encourage telling tales out of school. It means that they know you are approachable and will listen and talk to them. An adult's viewpoint and encouragement is often all it takes to put the trauma of a childhood skirmish into perspective, so that your child can move on.

A Strategy for Running a Family Meeting

People say things that are not true, circumstances arise that are easy to misinterpret, and outright lies flood our society. For children to survive this cultural chaos, they must learn to cut to the heart of every matter, and find the core of truth in what they hear, what they feel, and what they observe.

William and Candice Backus, 'Teaching Your Children to Tell Themselves the Truth'

A STRATEGY FOR RUNNING
A FAMILY MEETING

⊗ Spin a mustard bottle or draw straws for who will be chairperson.

⊗ Use the pepper mill (or something similar) and give each child, as well as mum and dad, a turn to hold it and speak.

⊗ Begin with fun—let everyone tell: the funniest thing that happened during the week, one thing they would invent that would make the world a better place, one thing they would save if the house was on fire, one thing they would like to do in the next month, or something similar.

⊗ Talk about one issue that Mum and Dad want to talk about and one issue that each child would like to talk about. (Use the pepper mill again.)

⊗ Work out solutions that everyone can live with, and draw up a contract.

⊗ Talk about penalties and rewards for keeping the contract. Don't forget to collect signatures on the document, so that they learn the importance of agreements!

⊗ If you are running a meeting about the family chores, draw jobs out of a hat. Your children will be delighted to see you drawing a chore. They think they have to do everything!

A family meeting should be the centrepiece of your family life. Fathers, it is your chance to instigate the most important meeting of the week.

Teams have meetings, schools have staff meetings and businesses have team meetings. Your family is the crucial unit of society, so why not have a weekly family meeting?

As has been said before, while children are good observers, they are not so good at interpreting what they see, so it is vital that you are there to talk things over and help interpret what is going on for them. They will sometimes tell you, in the course of a family meeting about bullying at school or communicate a false interpretation of a situation. Adults are there to interpret for children.

Older children will learn to give their view of things to a younger child and suggest ways of sorting matters out. Family meetings develop co-operation and loyalty and reassure the family of your commitment.

You will be able to solve problems with the family, hear about their hassles, and give them some skills to negotiate those day-by-day interactions that make up our lives. It will

117

also be your chance to hand on some "generational wisdom"—and you might even do some "growing" yourself!

When a child brings an issue to the table—lack of respect for his belongings by other family members, for instance—or wants to negotiate the family rules, then we sometimes have to look at ourselves. It is always worth seeking a win–win situation with your kids. Remember, the truth will set you free, even if it cheeses you off when you first hear it!

We sometimes have to deal with our own issues before we can expect our children to deal with theirs. I am of Scottish descent, and found it very easy to 'put porridge on everyone' (lose it!) when I was frustrated about something. However, before I could expect my family to address anger in a healthy way, I had to look at myself, and then as a family we were able to work out some strategies. (See 'A Strategy for Addressing Anger'.)

A family meeting can be held regularly—same time, same day, every week. It is a good idea to give each of the children a turn at organising it and maybe choosing the dinner that night.

A family meeting should do any or all of the following:

- ✪ Review the week.
- ✪ Celebrate anything good that has happened that week.
  (You can present accolades. They only need to be simple things—a stamp on a card, a chocolate fish or something similar.)

- ✪ Organise fun and recreation times.
- ✪ Air gripes.
- ✪ Make contracts for change.
- ✪ Decide on chores.

Holding the pepper mill when it is their time to speak helps each child (and the adults!) feel important and listened to.

RULES FOR HOLDING THE PEPPER MILL

The speaker holds the pepper mill to make a request. He has to:

- ✪ have the right expression (non-critical) on his face as he relays the request, and
- ✪ explain the problem clearly and simply, and
- ✪ tell how he will feel if that request is understood.

The chairman repeats the request while the speaker still has the pepper mill. The speaker only hands the pepper mill on when he feels he has been heard correctly, and then he passes the pepper mill to others to share their feelings on the matter. In this communication it is important that when people share, they don't mind read or rebut; they just tell how they feel. For example, the speaker cannot say things like: 'Dad, you're always knocking my music, because you're from another generation!' Rather: 'I feel you do not appreciate the music I like!'

Dad, enjoy your role as the coach. Keep on inspiring the team and negotiating solutions that you can all live with.

A STRATEGY FOR DADS WHO REGULARLY COME HOME AFTER THE CHILDREN ARE IN BED

Son, I don't care if the basement wall is cracked. Please stop telling everyone you come from a broken home!

Author unknown

A Strategy for a Dad Who Regularly Comes Home after the Children Are in Bed

✪ Give each of your children a special exercise book. Tell them that it is their own 'Dad's Book' — i.e. Johnny's Dad's book. It's a book in which you and the child write messages to each other every day.

✪ Ring your children from work sometime after school just for a chat. Take the opportunity (if you need to) to remind them to write down their message for you.

✪ When you arrive home, go to their bedrooms to kiss them and collect the books. Then at some stage in the evening, write your own special message to your children in the books. Your message can be an expression of love, a fatherly message that you want him to always remember, a response to something he has told you— or for a small child, just a picture. Your artistic efforts will be appreciated! It will probably be the first thing each child reads in the morning.

✪ Occasionally, just for fun, if they are still awake, pop the kids into the car, still in their pyjamas, and take them to a drive-through 'takeaway' and shout them a milkshake or whatever they would like. Tell them it is because they are the best members of your team!

✪ Make it a ritual to say a blessing over your children each night. Even if they are asleep.

Dad, is God a Power Ranger? Dad, why do dogs chase cats? Dad, the kids at school call me four-eyes. These are the questions and worries that small people need to run past their parents. Unfortunately these questions don't often come to the surface while you are watching TV or rushing out the door to make a meeting.

Busy fathers face a big challenge in finding focused time with their children. Remember, children don't need your total constant attention, but they will thrive on at least short spurts of focused attention.

Build time for your children into your schedule. If you arrive home late regularly, try to make time in the weekend. For instance, have a Sunday morning tradition of giving the family breakfast in bed. Use biscuit cutters to cut the toast into shapes and call it Dad's toast. Or make it a tradition that on holidays, Dad makes pancakes for the family.

Let your child get into bed with you and read his Dad's Book entries for the week. Set a bedtime for your children half an hour earlier than necessary and allow them to use this time to write in the book or read. Let them ring you up (if this is feasible) before they go to sleep.

123

When you are home, have a ritual of carrying them into bed in different ways. You can use a fireman's hold, or they can walk on your feet, ride on your back etc. A friend with four-year-old twin boys asked them, at the end of a big week which included their birthday party, 'What was the nicest thing that happened this week?' They both replied, 'When Daddy bounced us into bed.'

Sit on the end of your children's beds and ask them to tell you one thing that they are thankful for this week. Then tell them one thing that you are thankful for.

As long as your children know there will be some "Dad" time, they will be fine. It may be while you are shaving, it may be while you are driving—it doesn't matter when or where, as long as there is a time when you find it easy to talk to your children.

Create a ritual such as a "date" with one of your children each month. Ring your child up from work and invite him to join you at a restaurant for Saturday breakfast. Even a two or three-year-old will think a date—on their own!—with their father is magic. Take turns with your child in choosing the venue.

Use the opportunity of the "date" to tell your child how proud you are of the person that she or he is growing up to be. Ask about teachers and friends. Ask what was the best thing that happened this week and what was the worst thing.

Even a teenager who may be going through the "cave men-tality" stage (when they spend a lot of time hiding in their bedroom) will respond to a date if it is an established part of your family tradition. By then it may be more sophisticated, like an outing to buy a piece of sports equipment or to a concert.

Send a note to your child. Be a big spender. Put a stamp on it and really mail it!

Give your children the time they need and learn to converse with them and learn to ask the sort of questions that will open their souls. Questions such as the following will tell you a lot about what is going on in your child's head:

- ❂ If you could invent one thing that would make the world a better place, what would it be?
- ❂ What would be the first thing you would do if you were Prime Minister?
- ❂ What qualities do you want in a friend?
- ❂ What do you think heaven is like?

Turn the television off (or at least turn the sound off) or put down the newspaper when your children are talking to you. They need to know that what they have to say is important to you.

However, remember that once you have given children some quality attention, you can set the boundaries and establish your need for quietness and space, too. One of the greatest needs of busy people is the need for some tranquillity at home. It is fine for you to say, 'Now it is my time to have quietness and for you to read the paper, watch television …'

A STRATEGY FOR
STAYING IN TOUCH
WITH YOUR CHILDREN

*Feeling loved, understood, and paid attention to by parents
helps teenagers avoid high-risk activities regardless of whether
a child comes from a one or two parent household.*

US National Longitudinal Study of Adolescent Health,
1997

A Strategy for Staying in Touch with Your Children

✪ Sit on the end of the bed and ask your child three questions:
'What was the nicest thing that happened to you today?'
'What was the yukkiest thing that happened?'
'What is one thing that you're thankful for today?'
Then tell them one thing that you're thankful for.

✪ Try to sit down to breakfast with your family, and try to have a "team talk" before everyone goes out the door.

✪ Plan some landmark events in your child's life—a weekend away with you and your spouse and each child on their tenth birthday, for instance.

✪ Establish a hobby or practise a skill with your 5 to 10 year-olds. Teach them woodworking, sporting skills, house maintenance—something they show an interest in.

Recent research—a Federal study in the USA known as the National Longitudinal Study of Adolescent Health (the largest of its kind ever conducted, involving 90,000 12- to14-year-olds), published in 1997—identified strong emotional connection with parents as the factor that best protected young people from high-risk behaviour. It concluded, as I quoted above, that 'Feeling loved, understood, and paid attention to by parents helps teenagers avoid high-risk activities regardless of whether a child comes from a one or two parent household'.

It also concluded that children whose parents are home at key times of the day—at breakfast, after school, at dinner, at bedtime—are less likely to try alcohol, tobacco or marijuana. Apparently, when parents are available to talk to them, adolescents' emotional stress is reduced, making them less likely to engage in early sex, experiment with drugs and alcohol, commit suicide, or behave violently.

Strong emotional attachments with our children tend to be formed through the small day-to-day interactions, in the same way that a coach builds trust through good and bad times. You may not be able to be home at dinnertime or bedtime every night, but you can plan some ways of keeping that connection.

Pick your children up whenever possible from sports events or parties.

Practise questions such as 'Tell me two things that happened today and how you felt about them.'

Use questions like:

- ✪ What?
- ✪ How?
- ✪ Could?

Avoid using 'Why' questions—they usually get a conversation stuck.

When your teenager wants to talk, try to discipline yourself to hang around and listen. It can be inconvenient and you may be bone tired, but when they want to sit on the end of your bed and talk after a school event or party, try to stay awake. The moment may not be recaptured. A listening ear from you when they need it is your best ally during the teenage years.

Plan 'landmark' events for your children. For example, you could instigate a tradition of a weekend away with you the summer following your son's twelfth birthday. This special event will be something your son looks forward to throughout his childhood, and looks back on for the rest of his life. The emerging adolescent can choose where you go: it may be a camping ground, a canoe safari or a tramping trip.

The plan is to create a sort of 'men's weekend' away when you can talk about growing up, relationships with the opposite sex, the kind of man he wants to be—and you can answer his questions. This is their initiation into puberty. You can play tapes and discuss them late into the night.

For your daughter, you may decide that a weekend trip with mum and dad for her tenth birthday, when she chooses where you go and what you do, will be the best way to give her some quality time with you before she hits the stormy years of puberty.

I spent my early parenting years totally involved in running youth programs, which meant that I was out most evenings during the week, not to mention the weekends. In those days, I was intent on changing the world, and was determined that I would use every spare minute "making a difference"!

As far as my wife, Mary, was concerned, it really did make a difference—particularly to the load she had to carry with the children. It finally clicked with me that some changes would have to be made if I was going to stay in touch with my kids—and in the good books with Mary!

The change I made is one that has been the foundation of our family. It has had so many positive spin-offs that it would be hard to estimate the value to our family of our breakfasts together.

I was naturally a morning person, and Mary was definitely an "owl". So I decided I would get up early, take the dog for a run and prepare breakfast. This gave Mary time to help the children dress, make beds and pack schoolbags. We all then sat down together while I read a short Bible story to the family, followed by three or four questions.

The value of the reading and discussion before the family attacked their day was inestimable. The children had a chance to talk about any worries they had concerning the day, we communicated about each other's schedules, and the family "team talk" set the tone for the day. The other benefit was that by orchestrating some quiet "sitting down" time before we all left the house, there was less chance of anything being left behind!

We recently had a family celebration during which we asked the children to share their favourite childhood memory. Because verbosity is in the genes in our family, they found it hard to share only one memory! But each listed those breakfasts near the top, amongst their family treasury of best memories.

When our children were nearing the end of primary school, we moved cities. The house that we shifted to had only a breakfast bar and a formal dining room. However, within a few weeks we had decided, as a family, to invest in a kitchen table. We were missing the breakfasts together. During such a vulnerable time as a change of citiy, that morning family time was especially important.

Children of the new millennium, when change is likely to continue and stress will be inevitable, are going to need, more than ever, the mentoring of an available father.

It is a skill to know how to manage all the roles that make

up being a father—you have to stay something of a hero, and stay calm, and stay in charge, and remain friends with your children!

Building the friendship while still establishing and maintaining limits on your children's behaviour will be easier to do when you are involved in their lives. There will be times when a developing child or teenager, unskilled in handling relationships, may cross the barrier or wobble a little on a corner. This is part of their learning curve. They may, at times, disappoint you and hurt you with thoughtless actions and words. This usually stems more from their immaturity and lack of skill in handling relationships with adults than from any great dislike for you.

It is the way you react when a child messes up that will give him the tools to cope with life as he grows up.

You may identify your parenting style and perhaps have to modify your reactions if you find yourself locked into power struggles or just being ignored by your children. (Check out the parenting models in the chapter on 'Discipline for Dads'.)

Imagine your eight-year-old child is allowed to use your tools to build a wooden boat. You come home two days later and find your best saw lying on the lawn going rusty.

- ✪ The parentus sergeant majorcus races inside and yells, 'You stupid twit! That's the last time you're ever going to use my tools. You know the rules! That's it! Get out of here!'
- ✪ The parentus jellyfishicus would come in and say,

'Don't worry, dear, I'll buy another saw. It's good that you're being so creative.'

○ And the parentus backbonicus? He is likely to come in and say, 'Now look what I found on the drive. You've got a problem. But here's some steel wool—this will need some elbow grease and some oil. Off you go now, and have a go at cleaning it up. If you need a hand, come and get me.' This father knows that he could clean up the saw in a fraction of the time. He knows that he'll probably have to do it again anyway. But he sees it as chance for his child to learn how to own problems and solve them.

What is going to happen in fifteen years' time, when the kids of these different parenting styles have adult-sized problems?

○ The child of the parentus sergeant majorcus will lock up with paralysis. Inside, this person will still hear the yelling, even if no one is yelling in the real world. He or she will feel bad, and might reach for anything that will take away the pain—a bottle, a pill, maybe a knife.

○ The child of the parentus jellyfishicus will just walk away from it. 'Oh dear, what a mess. Someone else can sort that out.' Work hassle or a relationship problem, it won't matter; this person will just run away.

○ But the child of the parentus backbonicus will say, 'Hmmm ... I've got a problem. It's my problem, but I can solve it. There are no problems so big that they can't be solved.'

TEACH A SKILL

Wynton Rufer, the champion soccer player, recently told me that in Germany and South America, even a seven-year-old would be able to keep a soccer ball in the air up to 500 times, whereas he hasn't found a seven-year-old in Australia or New Zealand who can do it. When our children are young, and teachable, and long for our company, we can tune in on the opportunity to give them some of the skills and confidence that will be a platform for their future.

In the USA, children of that age—whose heroes are basketball players such as Michael Jordan—can dribble a basketball magnificently, because they have had some inspiration and because they practice.

Sport can be a very useful "safe" subject.

Buy a second-hand yacht, go-kart or bike for your child, and let the child help you bring it up to standard. One teenager said, 'Dad and I always played cricket together. When we couldn't talk about much without sparks flying, we could always talk about cricket.' It was a "safe" subject for many years, and it gave them a place to connect!

A STRATEGY FOR
LISTENING TO YOUR
TEENAGE DAUGHTER

A girl's father is the first man in her life, and probably the most influential. Absent or involved, loving or rejecting, what he is or was leaves a lasting imprint.

David Jeremiah, Author and Counsellor

A STRATEGY FOR LISTENING TO YOUR TEENAGE DAUGHTER

Be involved with your daughters. Admire them. Teach them self-sufficiency. Respect their space and never evaluate their looks, except positively.

✪ Ask your daughter about three things that happened today and how she feels about them.

✪ Ask your daughter who would her ideal man be?

✪ Ask your daughter about what dreams she has for her future.

A father has a tremendous impact on how his daughter views herself. If a father sees his daughter as intelligent, capable and attractive, she will also see herself that way.

A father's approval of his teenage daughter defines her identity and worth, as well as her sense of the possibilities in her own life and of her ability to achieve her goals.

A number of recent research essays into eating disorders shows that if a father comments on his daughter's tendency to be overweight, she will have twice the risk of an eating disorder, than if a mother makes the same observation.

When a girl reaches adolescence, she looks to her father for approval and love. If he is not available to her, she will look to some other male to fill the gap. There is something in masculine affirmation that female affirmation does not contain. Model positive masculinity; let her experience what a proper, respectful male response sounds and feels like.

In a recent research study, a doctoral student looked at the bereavement patterns of twenty adolescent girls whose fathers had recently died. One question the researcher asked was what they would miss most about their fathers. One of the answers that showed up repeatedly was that they would especially miss their fathers when problems arose or questions came up. They would often wonder, 'If Dad were here now, what would he say?' That is not surprising. One of the unique qualities of fathers is their task orientation; they solve problems. They restore order to their child's world.

I was explaining to parents at a parenting evening the importance of talking and listening to your teenage daughter, and suggested that a useful tool to get them talking was to ask the same question your wife might like you to ask her. That is, 'Tell me three things that happened today and how you feel about them.'

The following evening a father came up to me smiling broadly and said, 'That idea really worked! I have four daughters at high school and when I got home last night my eldest daughter was still up. She asked what I had learned at a "parenting course", with an adolescent sneer in her voice. I remembered what you said and just kept my cool. I asked her, "How about you tell me three things that happened today and how you feel about them?" I was amazed. She sat down and began to talk. In fact, three-quarters of an hour later she was still talking. I had to suggest that it was time for bed, but she insisted on playing me a song that she had written that day, on the guitar.'

He continued, 'Considering that we hadn't had a proper conversation for months—just grunts—that was a miracle. I'm definitely going to practise the question thing. I've got three more teenage girls to try it out on!'

Remember, the relationship becomes very important during the teenage years, and the atmosphere between you and your teenage daughter is vital. Letting go your control, as she takes more responsibility for her own life, will let you assume the role of the mentor—coach, which is what she needs during this time. When she rings you from a party, or calls you when she has crashed your car, she won't be wanting a lecture or someone to tell her what a loser she is. She will already be very aware of her problem. She'll be looking for a father she can trust to be there for her when she needs him.

We need to flatter and admire our daughters, but never invade their space or exploit them. Our daughters need to practise conversation and mutual admiration with a safe male, and we can be that safe male. By both listening and talking to her, she will gain self-assurance, and so will not need the approval of the first boy who comes her way.

Respect her space, but try to connect whenever possible. If your daughter feels free to talk to you about what's really going on, knowing that this will not bring on a lecture, then she is likely to stay out of serious trouble most of the time.

Talk to your daughter in the car, as you're driving her places. Talk about current television shows, or what she thinks about certain current affairs issues or news items. Ask her about the music she listens to. About the messages that come through and what she thinks about them. She will learn good judgement by you asking her to use it.

Always remember to ask, 'How did it make you feel when . . .?'

Since your daughter gains security from how you see her, here are some ways to begin a conversation with your teenage daughter about drugs or alcohol (but obviously the same strategy works for boys, too):

- ✪ You are more important to me than you will ever believe. If I had information that might keep you alive, would you be interested in hearing about it?
- ✪ What would you say to kids who try marijuana or alcohol?
- ✪ What do you think it does for them to use drugs?
- ✪ Can you tell me how you say 'no' sometimes, in a way that works for you? How do you do that?

Here are some conversation openers about sexual choices:

- ✪ What sort of person do you want to one day marry?
- ✪ How do you think you will recognise the right person?
- ✪ Do you think that love and sex are the same?
- ✪ I was really surprised to learn that the most often asked question from girls is how to say no to their boyfriend without hurting his feelings. What do you think about this? When do you think it is OK to have sex? What are your values on this subject?
- ✪ Do you think a lot of teenagers are going to regret, later on, the sexual choices they made?

Explain to your teenage daughter that you don't expect her to be sexually active. Your high expectations of her will be her best protection. Explain that you want this for her because you love her and don't believe that teenage boys are capable of the commitment that goes with sexual activity. Talk about her dreams and the gift of faithfulness that she will give her future life-partner by setting boundaries on her friendships. Explain that a girl who has personal boundaries is very attractive to the opposite sex, that within those boundaries there is the opportunity to explore all sorts of friendships, enjoying each other's personalities and being creative in doing things together. Explain that this way she will give herself the option of backing out of a friendship without any of the embarrassment, complications or the emotional pain that result from sexual involvement.

But most of all, explain the beauty of a committed relationship and the long-term fulfilment and stability that being married to a man of character will bring to her life.

If your teenage daughter breaks up with her boyfriend, take her to dinner and let her know that there's a man in her life who will always love and accept her.

Finally, let her know, in no uncertain terms, that no future 'beau' will ever be good enough for her, in your eyes. Affirm that, as far as you are concerned, she is tops, and that you have confidence in her ability to make good decisions about her own life. I remember reading an article in the *Australian Women's Weekly* (6 July 1996) about Dawn French. When Dawn was an overweight 14-year-old about to go to her first disco, her father sat her down for a talk. She expected the usual father–daughter spiel about boys with high testosterone levels. He did spell out what he'd do to any over-enthusiastic lad who dared lay a finger on her. But what he said next has stayed with her forever.

He told her she was the most precious thing in his life, uncommonly beautiful, that he prized her above everything and was proud to be her father. No father could have given his daughter a more valuable start. Instead of approaching adolescence as the fat girl without a boyfriend, Dawn knew she was loved for who she was, not what she looked like. That confidence remained, and she has become the star of several popular television series including *French and Saunders*, *Murder Most Horrid* and *The Vicar of Dibley*.

'How wise of my father to say that,' reflected Dawn. 'How could you not be well-equipped to deal with life when you felt so loved and supported?'

Fathers, we are important. If you are a 'waster', she may end up marrying someone similar and try to rescue him, because she really wanted to rescue you.

A STRATEGY FOR
BUILDING FRIENDSHIP
WITH YOUR SONS

You're not a man until your father says you're a man.

Burt Reynolds

A STRATEGY FOR BUILDING FRIENDSHIP WITH YOUR SONS

✪ Children love to get down on the ground and play-rough and tumble. Boys, especially, will benefit from a father's physical involvement with them. Remember, for boys, the game is more important than the relationships. Boys will rarely stop the game because of an argument. They will sort it out and get on with it.

✪ Play wrestling is a great way for fathers to teach sons how to fight without harm. Let him enjoy the long struggle—until the final giving in, "calling it quits" and admitting he lost. Let your son win occasionally, but make sure you aren't a pushover.

✪ Teach your son how to be a good winner and a good loser, and teach him how to use physical strength without dominating and hurting. Play fighting will help your son learn to control himself, a skill that will be vital for him as he heads into the emotion-filled years of adolescence.

✪ Fatherly affection, be it an arm around the shoulder or a friendly wrestle, along with consistent discipline, are also vital, and help sons grow up to be manly men with good social skills.

✪ Organise an annual Lads and Dads weekend for you and your sons.

A Catholic nun who worked in a men's prison in the USA was asked by one of the inmates if she would buy him a Mother's Day card to send to his mum. She agreed. Word of this travelled fast and soon hundreds of inmates were asking for cards. The resourceful nun contacted a greeting card manufacturer, who obliged with crates of Mother's Day cards, all of which she passed out.

Soon afterwards, she realised that Father's Day was approaching. Thinking ahead, she again called the card manufacturer, who responded with crates of cards.

Years later, the nun said she still had every one of those Father's Day cards! Not one prisoner requested a card for his father. She said, 'Clearly men in prison lack fathers.'

As fathers, we need to communicate with our sons.

Your children will most want to please you when they are between six and eight years of age. During that period between infancy and adolescence, children are very teachable. When a boy reaches six, he becomes a male-role-model-seeking missile. This is when he needs a father to teach him what it is to be a man. During those years he wants to be around men and boys, so we have this window of opportunity to teach skills and build friendship. Boys, particularly feel secure if they know:

- ✪ Who's in charge?
- ✪ What are the rules?
- ✪ Will the rules be enforced fairly?

DO STUFF WITH YOUR SONS

The path to closeness with sons is activity together. Be available, and be interested in spending time with your boys. Doing things with them, challenging and testing them.

This is where your leadership comes to the fore. It is your privilege to teach your son how to throw a ball, how to stand up to bullies at school, and that it's an honourable thing to hold a job.

I love the story of Henry Luce (founder of Time/Life Inc.), whose publications probably influenced world opinion more than any others in history. Luce (a missionary's son) frequently reminisced about his boyhood in China. In the evenings, he would go for long walks outside the compound with his father, who would talk to him as if he were an adult. The problems of administering a school and the philosophical questions occupying him were all grist for their conversational mill. Their bond was tight, because they were friends—and both father and son were nourished by the relationship.

In many tribal societies, at about fourteen years of age, boys were initiated into manhood through an initiation ceremony which often involved many challenges. After this, a boy was identified with the men of the village or tribe. Boys look for challenge and adventure at this age; unfortunately, our world, with its focus on schooling, education, exams and careers, doesn't offer many such opportunities to this age group apart from sport. That is why your sons need a variety of activities, such as fishing, camping, fixing things, and sport, as well as being given genuine responsibilities. Young people were made for challenges. Boys especially need to be challenged to do something significant with their lives. Although adolescence is generally a time of self-absorption, it is also a time of sorting through who they are and what they believe in.

At around fourteen years of age, there is usually a period when adolescents have a tremendous sense of the possibilities of their future and a great belief in their own potential. If we don't capitalise on that, and instead rip them off with materialism or allow sexual permissiveness, then that's what they will settle for. By the time they reach sixteen or seventeen, that window of opportunity has closed.

When I led a youth organisation in New Zealand involving thousands of teenagers in weekly clubs, the voluntary staff used to comment that when teenagers got involved at the beginning of their fourth form year (at approximately fourteen years old) they tended to stay with the club program throughout their high school years. If they didn't get involved in that year, they rarely joined later; cynicism had settled in by about fifteen or sixteen years of age.

Even if your sons are successful in many different academic and sporting activities, let them know that you are as proud of their willingness to take leadership roles and to serve in unnoticed ways, as you are in their achievements.

This is where the coach can have his finest hour. How you handle your moody fourteen-year-old son may set the tone of your relationship with him for the rest of his life. However, patience is a wonderful thing. When I was sixteen I thought my father knew very little. By the time I was twenty-one I was amazed at how much he'd learned in five years!

Freud says adolescence is a temporary mental illness—but it need not be if there is a mentor that will step in and fill the gap. Teenage boys do need a male mentor who will inspire them. Sadly, this need often coincides with a time when their relationship with their father is the pits!

There is some frightening research from Australia: nearly a third of men never speak to their father. Another third only use "put downs", or mock their fathers when speaking to them. The final third have merely "distance" talk: about sport, power tools etc. Only one in twelve sees his father as an emotional support.

CONNECTING WITH YOUR ADOLESCENT

During adolescence, many things change in your relationship with your son. He is now very aware of his ability to think for himself, and that's just what he wants to do. He will tend to push you away and become difficult if you try to keep too much control. So the relationship becomes the most important factor, and the atmosphere between you is the area on which you need to concentrate.

Who is your adolescent son? You will find out by learning

to understand how he feels and what he thinks about issues affecting him. It is all about him. Not about you, the family, or anybody else. An adolescent will not allow you into his feelings unless he trusts you. He needs to believe that you will support him and not ridicule, belittle, moan at, or control him when he shares himself.

The best way to work on building this trust is by using a technique called "mirroring". A mirror tells what it sees. It doesn't tell us what to do. It leaves it up to us to decide what to do with the information it shows us.

It is hard sometimes for parents to hold back from giving teenagers advice, but if we truly want to be mentors, we have to check ourselves constantly to ensure that we stay in the role of guide.

If you feel you have lost touch with your teenage son, try to connect in some way. Ask if he'd like to come along when you go on a trip, perhaps, or suggest a run, a game of tennis etc. Read his body language, then try to work out what you are seeing and put a name to it. You might say something like:
'You look down.'
'You sound frustrated.'
'You look happy.'

If he is despondent for some reason, try identifying the feeling: 'You look wasted. Can I get you a Coke?' You could then sit down and ask: 'Do you want to talk about it?' If he agrees, use the four-question approach:

- ✪   What happened?
- ✪   How do you feel?
- ✪   What do you think?
- ✪   What are you going to do about it?

A mother once asked me what her estranged husband could do to try to reconnect with his teenage son. She said, 'My son says that he hates him.' The husband had instructed his wife that he would be there to pick up his son and he expected her to make sure the kid came. The mother knew that there was no way she could or would force her son to go with his father, but she also knew that her son needed his father's influence in his life. I suggested that she explain to her husband that it might be much better to buy a couple of milkshakes and hamburgers, invite the boy to sit on the front lawn while they ate them, and say something like, 'This isn't working, son. What can we do to make it work?'

There are numerous opportunities to read your adolescent's body language all day long. Try looking for them. If your teenager allows you into his feelings, he will allow you into his thinking; as a friend and mentor you can then help guide his choices.

Teach your son that it's all right for a man to ask for nurturing, help, support and healthy affection. Let him know how much you value your friendships and partnerships. Tell him that the notion of the self-made man is a myth.

To paraphrase Steven Covey, the best-selling author of Seven Habits of Highly Effective People—teach him how to communicate for the purpose of understanding, not just to get his point across or to win an argument.

In Western society, boys are doing badly, especially at school, compared with their sisters. The "it's cool to be a fool" syndrome keeps many of our intelligent and capable boys locked into acting dumb. They are reluctant to do anything that will mark them out as different from their mates. For example, the skipper of *The Spirit of Adventure*, an old-fashioned sailing ship that gives young people a month-long "on the edge" experience, was quoted as saying that he has no trouble getting young female crews, but struggles to get teenage boys. This would not have been the case ten years ago.

We can rise to the challenge to unlock our young people from the "act dumb" syndrome. We fathers definitely need to take steps to make peace with our sons.

A Strategy for Getting to Know Your New Baby

Fatherhood took me by surprise. Something happened in my soul when I held my own baby for the first time.

Words of a proud first-time Dad

A Strategy for Getting to Know Your New Baby

Often your baby doesn't want toys. Your baby wants you, made by God, and batteries not included.

✪ Talk to your newborn baby as much as possible. Hold your baby in your arms often. Talk as if your baby understands every word you say—cricket will do fine!

✪ Sing and dance with your new baby. Encourage your baby to touch and feel safe and clean objects—spoons, soft toys, rattles, a ball, keys—keys are always favourites. Kneel down and talk to your baby. Listen with your eyes.

✪ Get on the floor and play "dad games". Wrestling and rough and tumble games are dad specialties.

✪ Help care for your new baby. Help with feeding, nappy changing, bathing, dressing, pram pushing.

✪ Read to your new baby.

✪ Affirm your wife as a good mother. Her smile and her sense of wellbeing will be the reflection that your baby absorbs as his security.

Mothers parent differently from fathers. Some video studies of parenting behaviour show that mothers spend most of their time with the new baby doing what are described as "caring" jobs—bathing and feeding and changing and cuddling—while fathers spend more time playing with the baby. Mostly the only way fathers know how to babysit is by being a playmate.

Infants learn through play. Newborn babies can see, hear, smell and respond to touch but only dimly—what actually 'wires' a child's brain (or rewires it after trauma) is repeated experience. Each time a baby tries to touch a tantalising object, or gazes intently at a face, or listens to a lullaby, tiny bursts of electricity shoot through the brain, knitting neurons into circuits, as well-defined as those etched onto silicon chips.

Walk around the house and the garden showing your baby different objects and letting her feel the textures of different surfaces. Sing and dance with your baby. She will love your deep voice and more boisterous play.

The physical dimension and contact of a father/son relationship, especially, is important. Think of how we love to toss our infant or toddler son up in the air. He is kind of scared, but because we are laughing, he is laughing too, even though he is not so sure he feels like laughing.

Often our wives or partners watch us doing this and almost have a heart attack. But this kind of play is part of the pattern of masculine bonding. When a father does this, he is teaching his infant son that what is scary (but not too risky) can also be fun. This is a characteristic of masculinity. If we as a father, laugh with our tiny son as we toss him in the air, he will get the message, 'This should be fun'.

So we fathers can relax and do what comes naturally. Observe your baby closely several times a day. Bath him. Listen to his gurgles; even if you're changing a nappy, concentrate on his smiles, not just on the mess. Roll around the floor with him. You'll want to stop and play—quick before he changes!

Children who don't play much, or who are rarely touched, develop brains 20 to 30 per cent smaller than normal for their ages.
('Fertile Minds', *Time* Magazine 3 February 1997.)

A STRATEGY FOR
A MEN'S WEEKEND WITH
YOUR PRE-TEENAGE SON

*I feel like a mosquito in a nudist colony. I know what I'm
supposed to do, but I just don't know where to begin.*

Author unknown

A STRATEGY FOR A MEN'S WEEKEND WITH YOUR PRE-TEENAGE SON

Plan together where you will go and what activities you will do. Camping, fishing or bushwalking are great comradeship builders. But if your son has a strong artistic inclination, he may prefer a weekend where you go to movies or an art gallery. What's important is that you plan it together and you do something you will both enjoy and learn from.

✪ Plan to take some tapes (either music or instructional) or just think about what you want to talk to your son about.

✪ Talk to him (and listen to him) about his goals and dreams for his future.

✪ Talk to him about your dreams of him growing into a man who gives manhood a good name. This isn't just about his career choice. This is about moral character—honesty, taking responsibility for his own behaviour, kindness, respect for others …

✪ Talk to him about friendship, and the qualities he can value in male friendships and in female friendships.

✪ Talk to him about his sexuality; spell out his responsibilities and privileges. He may not want to talk much, but he will listen.

✪ Tell him how proud you are of him and give him the messages he will need to internalise to see him through his teenage years.

✪ Ask him how he feels about becoming a man.

I love the story of the dad who planned a weekend away with each of his boys after their twelfth birthday. The plan was to create a sort of a "men's weekend" away, when they could talk about growing up, relationships with the opposite sex and generally enjoy an 'initiation' into manhood together. As they were planning this week, the subject of sex came up during a family discussion. The youngest boy (only seven) piped up and said, 'Yuk, I don't want to talk about that stuff ... Dad will tell me about that on our weekend!' There is no doubt that in this home, dad the coach was very much alive, and his young son knew he could trust his father to tell him what he needed to know for negotiating life, at the right time.

I believe that a weekend away with his father, at this stage of his life, will be landmark of initiation into manhood for your son as he heads into puberty, with all its challenges.

This is your opportunity to do some "men's things" together, and to talk over the hurdles and hopes that he can look forward to.

There is no doubt that forewarned is fore-armed, and giving your son some insights into the feelings and challenges of the testosterone-filled years ahead will stand him in great stead.

What are your dreams for your son? Do you want him to grow to be a man who gives manhood a good name? What are your son's dreams for himself? Do you know? How can you help make them come true?

Fathers need to be around, available and interested in sharing time with their sons.

There is a lot of male violence today. Much of it may be because males have not been given the tools to handle conflict or have lacked the secure, kind-but-firm father.

It is well known that males "flood" emotionally easily (their passions overflow), and that "macho-ness" has been associated with masculinity, when in fact the opposite is the case. Macho-ness can often be a cover for inadequacy in their emotional development.

According to Professor Eisikovits, director of the Minerva Centre for Youth Studies at the University of Haifa in Israel, 'Violence is not a behaviour, it is a way of looking at the world.' He also states that after twenty years, there is good research evidence to show that children who experience violence between their parents are far more seriously damaged psychologically than children who've been abused themselves.

Men need high cultural competency to perform well in groups, and some struggle with group competency because they are unable to express their emotions. They need good modelling and good mentoring from mature men.

Talking to your son on this weekend about his relationships with the opposite sex will be significant. Your high view of women, your love and respect for your wife, your daughters, your mother, your sisters will mould his view of women. Talk about the difference between sex and love, about personal boundaries and about commitment.

Use this time to talk about his dreams for the future, what he considers his life work might be. What his values are, the sort of person he would choose as a life partner etc. Allow him to identify those qualities that he values in a partner, and then ask him what qualities he wants to bring to a future marriage. Talk about his dreams, visions and goals. Let him know you believe in his ability to achieve his goals and talk about the strategies that will help him grow into a valuable human being with a strong character.

Talk about your faith and share some "coach" sayings. Things like: 'Life isn't always fair, but it's not what happens to you that counts; it's how you handle it that counts.'

Repeat this men-only recreational experience on a yearly basis.

A STRATEGY FOR
DATING YOUR
CHILD

*When I took my kid out to eat, she ordered the most
expensive thing on the menu—a big Mac with double cheese.*

Author unknown

A STRATEGY FOR
DATING YOUR CHILD

A date can be a regular monthly date with one child in the family, or it can be a date to play for a short spell of time, a trip to a sports event, or a shopping excursion together—with your credit card.

✪ Telephone your child from work and invite him or her out on a date. Or send a written invitation through the mail.

✪ If the date is for a meal out, let your child choose which restaurant—from a list of two or three restaurants you provide.

✪ Talk about the "date" for several days beforehand, dropping hints about what you are going to do etc.

✪ Have a "play date" with your child—10 minutes of concentrated attention.

✪ Plan something extra special relating to a particular interest your child has—a concert, sporting event, gallery opening.

We tend to live busy, high-speed lifestyles. But our kids deserve more than just our leftover time. Making a "date" reassures your child that he or she is a very important person in your life, and you have cleared some extra space in your timetable so you two can do something special together and enjoy each other's company.

The benefits of dating your children are immense. Over the years, you may not think that the time spent with your child and the conversations that you have are very significant. But when your son or daughter gets to the teenage years, and they want to talk something over, you have already built a tradition that keeps communication lines open.

It will also be some positive "built-in" time, time which is free from the (sometimes negative) emotions of adolescence. If you know that you have a date coming up, you can keep an issue that you want to talk to your son or daughter about until then, and address it in the relaxed and affirming atmosphere of your regular date.

Your date will give you the opportunity to keep in touch. Your child may want to unload a burden or just tell jokes and have a good time. As a safe father, who has listened to your child over many years, your familiarity will be welcome.

The following questions will help you open conversations on your date. Often a question is all it needs; from then on, your child will talk. Just the fact that you are interested in what he or she has to say is enough. Remember, ask questions that start with 'how' and 'what?', not 'why?' Here are some for starters:

- ✪ What are your dreams for your life?
- ✪ What are your goals for the next month?
- ✪ If you could have one wish come true, what would it be?

Play 'what if?'

- ✪ What would you do if you knew you could cure cancer, but it would cost you your life?
- ✪ What would you do if you discovered one of your friends was using marijuana?

Try to keep your dates fun. Choose to be cheerful and practise some questions to stay in touch with your child's world, but also remember that life is fun and funny.

Program (and remember to put it in your diary) a window of time each month when you date one of your children. This will mean that each child gets a date every few months (depending on the size of your family).

- ✪ Ring up your child from work and ask to arrange a time for a Dad's date.

- ✪ Schedule the date into the family calendar, and do not break it!
- ✪ Choose somewhere that is enjoyable for you both. You might take turns at choosing what you do. It can be a dessert, or a meal at their favourite restaurant, or an activity like video skud-racing, fishing or walking together.

"Play dates" work well if a child is whining for attention while you are trying to work. Let your child know when you'll be available (for example, after Play School or Sesame Street ends, or when the oven buzzer rings). At the appointed time, stop work and play hard for the agreed period of time. Many children are satisfied with a mere 10 minutes of concentrated play-date attention. Set the oven timer before you begin playing. When it buzzes, it will be the bad guy, making you go back to work!

Plan ahead for play dates, especially with older kids. To really honour your child, let the answering machine take all the calls during your play date.

Make sure that each child has a turn at play dates with you—if one child is trying to compete for your attention, you can remind the child that his or her turn will come.

Other ideas for dates:

- ✪ A shopping trip for one special item—a new part for an electric train, or a first soccer ball or netball.
- ✪ A picnic. Go with another father and one of his children. You could go to the park, the beach, a

football game, a car race, or go on a hike or a fishing trip.

- ✪ A lunch date or breakfast date. Send a written invitation through the mail.
- ✪ An excursion to do something your child has a special interest in—visit a dinosaur exhibition at the museum, go to a pop concert, fly a kite.

Our eldest son, from the age of about six, was fascinated by planes. He spent all his pocket money on books about planes, he got books out of the library and he wrote to the plane manufacturers for information. (He once sent an American dollar that I had given him to McDonnell Douglas telling them that he thought their planes were 'beaut', and received in return a huge parcel of promotional material. He knew facts and figures about planes that were astonishing.)

I managed to organise for a friend who worked at New Zealand's Ohakea airbase to show him around. The pilots and mechanics were fabulous to him: treating him like a man, letting him sit in the cockpit of a fighter plane and answering his questions. He came home with a much-treasured pilot's manual to add to his collection!

Another friend whose son was keen on sports cars wrote to several car dealers (who handle European sports cars) in a nearby larger city, asking if it would be possible to take one of their cars for a test drive, even though they were not going to buy. Several of the dealers wrote back and agreed, and the father and son had the time of their lives.

A STRATEGY FOR
AN EXPEDITION WITH
YOUR CHILDREN

The most urgent domestic challenge facing the United States at the close of the 20th century is the re-creation of father-hood as a vital social role for men.

David Blackenhorn, from the book *Fatherless America: Confronting Our Most Urgent Social Problem*

A STRATEGY FOR AN EXPEDITION WITH YOUR CHILDREN

✪ Have a vote about where you would like to go and how you would like to get there (maybe to a different city, by train).

✪ On the expedition, let each child have period of time during which he or she is in charge.

✪ Play family competitions such as card games on the train and plan the sights you will see.

✪ Let the child who has chosen the particular activity make decisions about who goes first and where you eat for that portion of the day.

In his book, *Fatherless America: Confronting Our Most Urgent Social Problem*, David Blackenhorn asserts that, 'The most urgent domestic challenge facing the United States at the close of the 20th century is the re-creation of fatherhood as a vital social role for men.' Studies in the USA and England show that between World War I and World War II, fathers spent an average of four hours per week with their children. After World War II, fathers spent an average of two hours a week with their children. By 1990, the amount of time had dropped dramatically—to seventeen minutes.

Although lifestyles vary, there is no doubt that because of the long hours many fathers now work, the amount of contact time with our children is unavoidably diminished from that of previous generations.

Therefore we need to compensate by taking "time out" for spurts of focused attention. One of the best ways to do this is through those time-honoured family traditions—dates, holidays and excursions.

In researching this book, I asked both children and fathers to tell about their favourite memories. I was invariably told that the best memories were of holidays and excursions that dad initiated and carried through. They all said how much they loved the fact that dad was available on holidays and excursions, and could then give them the sort of attention they often didn't get from him at other times.

The feedback reveals that children draw positively on the memories created when their father makes the effort to orchestrate a special event, and treasure for ever the memories of that fun time together, be it a day, a week or a month. The memories become like an exhibit in the museum of their own childhood as well as being "built in" to the subsequent traditions of the family.

A family friend of ours takes his family on an annual excursion. For each of the last three years, they have visited a main city and toured its significant sights. The rules are that they plan together where they would like to go, and then what sights they will visit. All the children are allowed to do some research and decide which attraction they want to be their part of the tour.

Dad decides on the mode of transport. Once he hired a four-wheel drive just for fun. Twice it has been the train. During the trip in the train, the children all have a segment of time when they decide (and organise) the entertainment—playing cards, alphabet games, 'what if?' etc.

If you visit a museum or an art gallery, give the children some challenges about what they must find. I remember taking an overseas speaker around some of the famous New Zealand tourist spots. He always knew something about the town that I didn't know, and had some place he wanted to go and see. I realised that he had done some quite thorough research before visiting, so he knew what to look for. Do the same with your children, and make the excursion into a sort of treasure hunt for the town's history—and then enjoy the kudos of being such a knowledgeable father!

Have an A, B, and C team for allocating seats—the team (family) members who are the first ready, and the best mannered, get to sit in the front seat.

If a family member can get a good deal from one of the attractions you visit, then he is allowed to spend what he saved on an edible treat to share with the others.

This sort of excursion helps you give your kids support while they are learning, a safe environment from which to explore the world, and a chance to try out their own ability in taking the lead.

Have fun for the few weeks after your expedition telling them what you enjoyed most, and asking them what their favourite place or time was. Then it's time to start planning the next expedition.

Today we do not know how to predict the world that our children will later be living in. So we will help our children best by encouraging them to become self-directed, so that they have a strong sense of who they are and why they are here, no matter what changes they have to deal with.

The family expedition will help them become self-directed human beings by teaching them life-skills.

A STRATEGY FOR
DISCIPLINE FOR
DADS

*Discipline is the process of teaching our children to think about
what they have done, and of giving them the tools to put it
right.*

A Strategy for Discipline for Dads

✪ The discipline enforced by fathers tends to have a longer-lasting effect than a mother's discipline. The healthy establishment of limits by a father fosters a boy's sense of masculinity and a girl's sense of security.

✪ Children must know that your total acceptance and love is not up for grabs, when you are dealing with their behaviour. They must know that you believe that they are good, generous and loving people and that you are addressing their behaviour—not their worth as people.

✪ Remember, the limits must be clear and the consequences communicated with reasons and without anger.

✪ Remember, choices equal consequences minus parental anger. If you get angry, the emotion will mask the opportunity to think clearly and the lesson will not be learnt.

✪ You must be consistent with your discipline if you want your children to believe in the consequences.

It has been said that we live in an age of child-like adults and adult-like children. You may remember the 1997 article in *Time* magazine that reported the flight of a seven-year-old across America. The father, it seemed, was vicariously trying to live his life through his little daughter. Tragically, the child and her father died while trying to land their plane in a storm. The article was entitled: 'Parents are supposed to be the grown-ups—aren't they?'

A *Sydney Morning Herald* article recently reported that if parents take their children shopping, the bill could increase by $70 to $80. Another recent article said that one in four children have hardly any fruit or vegetables in their diets.

It seems that parent-led families (families where parents are in charge and are not afraid to set boundaries for the good of their children) are in jeopardy—falling prey to the pressures of tiny tyrants and busy lifestyles.

The line of least resistance may be an attractive option in the short term, but in the long term it will not give your children the self-control or the respectful relationships that they will need to get on well in the world.

Those families that take the time to train their children to live within healthy boundaries, boundaries that are firm but fair, do themselves and their children a great favour.

Fathers, don't be afraid to discipline! Back up your wife or partner in this regard especially, by agreeing to agree in front of the children, and by modelling respect for women—never allow your children to speak disrespectfully to their mother. Have faith in your wife's ability to handle discipline situations and reinforce the fact that her decisions are as final as yours are, so that the children sense no inconsistency. Playing one parent off against the other is a popular ploy as soon as children detect a chink in the parental discipline armour.

Discipline is not the same as punishment. Discipline teaches children how they need to behave in order to fit into their family, their school, their community and their world. It is part of the socialisation process that shows children how to take responsibility for their own actions; it is a way of teaching them that other people have thoughts and feelings.

If, as a parent, you can do the job of separating the child from the behaviour, then you have probably pulled off the biggest coup of your life.

Your children need to know that they are 'pre-approved', and that your approval and love are not at stake. If you can send the message that you approve of them as people, even though you disapprove of some of (or at times lots of) their behaviour, then you are on track for a healthy, functioning family. But it's a hard act.

Many families operate on shame. Shame-based systems, where parents give love and acceptance on the basis of their children's performance, leave children empty inside. This sort of family may look the way it is meant to look (the kids are well-behaved), but because the children's needs are not being met, they are not operating on strength from the inside. The parents are controlling their behaviour through shame.

It is important that we are consistent, and understand that we are disciplining our children for the right reasons—to help them towards self-control and happiness. We can be secure about the quality of our child's character when we know that he can control his emotions and behaviour. Then whatever challenges he faces in life, he will respond to appropriately. Spoiled, indulged children tend to pay for their parents' indulgence in their adult years—and so will their parents, by having to deal with selfish, insecure and unprepared adults.

Discipline is about helping children make good choices, and about making it more comfortable for them to do the right thing and less comfortable when they choose to do the wrong thing.

We want our children to choose to tell the truth, so we can help them sort out any problems and find the best solutions. It is essential that children aren't afraid to tell parents the truth.

How often have you said (or heard a father say), 'Who did that?' Sometimes, fathers only want the answer to this question so they can make the child feel so bad, so small, so stupid or humiliated, that he won't do it again. That's shame, and shame doesn't work in the long run. Remember, dad is the big person, and when a dad tells a child what a 'dolt' he is, the child will probably believe it and live down to those expectations!

I used to ask my children the 'why?' question when they had done something wrong. 'Why did you do that?' or 'Why isn't that toy put away?' I then wondered why the communication got stuck. How can a child answer that question and win? What I really meant was. 'That toy needs to go away, son' or 'What happened here?' In this way the child could follow my instruction and put the toy away, or explain what had happened. Then it would be my turn, as the coach, to help the child put things right or sort the problem out.

Have you ever found one of your children standing there with a broken vase, a cricket bat and a sheepish look on his or her face? I would instinctively want to say, 'Who did that?' or 'Why did you do that?' and have a knee-jerk reaction to punish the offender.

But a much better way to find out the truth is to say, 'Now, guys, what happened here?' This lets them tell you what happened and take responsibility for their own actions. If you get angry and start yelling, you are more likely to put the children on the defensive and you will lose the opportunity for a lesson to be learned. They may tell you an imaginative story, which may not fit the facts (as you know them), in which case I suggest you wait, and go through the story with them. For instance: 'So the seagull flew in the window, broke the vase, flew out again, and left its cricket bat there! Is that the story?' After this, you may start to get close to the truth of the matter!

The reason for finding out the truth (the actual facts of the matter) is so that parents can give age-appropriate answers. You may say, 'OK then, now how are we going to make this right?' It may be by asking the children to clean up the mess and then pay for the vase out of their pocket money.

It is important that children aren't worried that, if they tell us the truth, we won't like them. Parents need to know the truth so they can hold children accountable for their behaviour; help them put it right and re-establish a clear conscience.

We want our children to feel strong; to learn how to act from strength on the inside.
 A parent coach needs to say 'yes' as often as possible. That may be:

- ✪   'Yes, now...' or
- ✪   'Yes, later...' or
- ✪   'Yes, after you have done your chores.'

A firm 'no' is just as important too, as children have to learn to live within family and social boundaries!

Unfortunately, many parents resort to nagging, yelling and blaming as a substitute for discipline. The child learns very little, except how to mimic your behaviour or, cynically, expect you to behave that way. The child in this situation often knows that he just has to wait while father blows his top, then he'll sort it out, pay the bill, buy a new one etc.

Because there are no real consequences for the child, the child doesn't need to change his behaviour. He just has to stand patiently while he is being yelled at!

Children are not born with natural self-control, your moral values and a propensity for co-operation. There are some children who are naturally compliant; they have lovely natures and are crushed by merely a stern look. These children grow up well-behaved and socialised, probably less because of great parenting than because they want to imitate and please their parents.

There are other children, however, who are not such willing learners. They will test their parents and the boundaries at every opportunity and despise you if you show weakness. I like to think of these children as spirited racehorses. They have spunk, personality and leadership. You just need to gain their respect, and give them the training and discipline their talent deserves, and you will end up with a winner—and a friend.

Fathers have a lot on their side when it comes to these "spirited" children if they can discipline themselves to stay calm and control their anger. In this situation, a father's objectivity will help the child think about what he must do when he crosses the line.

Remember, it's not the severity of the consequences that is important, but the certainty of them:

- ✪ Say it.
- ✪ Mean it.
- ✪ Do it.

The basic rule for discipline is to be consistent!

For small children, there are some other strategies that are very important to remember. They include:

- ✪ isolating the behaviour you don't want,
- ✪ practising the behaviour you do want,
- ✪ praising your children when they get it right.

HOW TO ISOLATE BEHAVIOUR YOU DON'T WANT

It is no fun sitting on the doorstep (if that is the place allocated to think about sulking), or being sent on an errand, when everyone else is having a good time. Children learn to behave in a certain way if they find that there is a pay-off for their behaviour. When we hardly notice their sulking, or quietly say, 'You may come and join the family when you have thought about what you need', they will learn that the effect of their behaviour on you is minimal, and they will be less likely to look for attention this way again.

Standing and thinking is a useful strategy. When your two-year-old openly defies your instruction to put away his toys, you can stand him in the corner while he thinks about what he should do. You can firmly say, 'Spitting on the wallpaper won't get you out of the corner. Saying silly words won't get you out of the corner. Just think about what will get you out of the corner.' Your two-year-old may think that he is going to stand there, like a soldier, for the rest of his life! However, seven or eight minutes is usually the limit he will hold out for!

Praise him when he agrees to co-operate. Having to sit in

the quiet-time chair for two minutes if he hits someone will teach your youngster that there are rules; after some thinking time, he knows he will be allowed to join the family again, and do whatever he has to do to sort out the problem.

HOW TO PRACTISE BEHAVIOUR YOU DO WANT

Remember that a big person coaching a small person is usually all the psychological power you need if you address issues at times you choose, instead of allowing the child to choose those times.

A child who does not behave well at kindergarten can be kept home for a day or two to practise behaving well. Cue— prompt—reinforce is a good formula. You can help him practise smiling and then going in the door and saying 'Hello' nicely to the teacher, before choosing what you are going to play at this morning. Practising smiling, going through the door and saying hello to the teacher gives him the security of knowing what behaviour is acceptable.

A child who will not go to his bedroom when his mother asks him to can learn very quickly that it is in his own interests to do so, if his father addresses the issue by making him practise the correct behaviour. When dad comes home he can suggest that they need to teach Johnny how to go to his room. Dad can then firmly supervise Johnny practising going to his bedroom—twenty times! This lesson is likely to stick, especially if it is carried out during Johnny's favourite television program. Again, his father's mere presence and deeper voice will often be all the back-up the child's mother needs to set a boundary on certain behaviour.

Children will repeat whatever behaviour gets them what they want, so never reward bad behaviour.

Discipline for children between five and ten years of age has a lot to do with training their consciences. They are learning right from wrong, and you have the chance, during these years, to teach them what they need to know.

Let the punishment fit the crime, and let them practise reparation whenever possible.

A friend who has a busy career in radio and television received a telephone call from a supermarket owner, in the middle of a video shoot, to say that her son had been caught stealing a Mars Bar. Her son had been given the option—either the police would be called, or his mother. He chose her! She immediately called a halt to what she was doing and rushed down to the shop. When she arrived, she thanked the owner for calling her, got her son to apologise and also suggested he think about what he could do to put the situation right with the shop owner. They agreed that he would spend an hour or so sweeping out the shop, stacking some boxes and, of course, that he would pay for the item. My friend thanked the shop owner, at which point he made a significant observation. He said, 'You know, you are the only parent who has ever come!'

Parents, be there to help children face their mistakes and bad choices and give them tools to put things right. Discipline is the process of training a child's conscience and helping the child link choices with consequences.

If a child consistently leaves his bike in the drive, denying him any televison viewing for a week doesn't necessarily make an appropriate link. But having his bike put away for a day will.

Discipline also teaches children that parents are to be respected and will, like benevolent dictators, enforce the boundaries in order to help their children grow into self-disciplined adults.

Discipline teaches children that there are limits, and that if they break these limits, their parents will notice and do something the children don't like. Your child may think, 'He's not going to beat me or scream or nag at me for hours. He'll deduct my pocket money, or I'll lose television or I'll be grounded or my curfew will be made earlier. Each of these is a pretty tough consequence individually, but if he uses all of them, it will really hurt. Maybe I'd be better off doing what he wants in the first place.'

For teenagers, there are some more specific strategies to add to the list. They include learning to:

- stop talking and start listening,
- co-operate,
- expect the best, and
- make deals.

Wouldn't it be great if you could freeze a fourteen-year-old and then thaw him out at eighteen? Sound attractive? No, not really. Think of all the fun you would miss out on during those years, and think of the lessons that your teenager has to learn during this period—it is a bit like a dress-rehearsal for life.

You see, for a teenager, the challenges are to start breaking away and start taking more responsibility for his or her own life. But teenagers still need your mature input, and they will achieve their goals with your support far more readily than they will if they sense that you are not prepared to let them break away healthily. Then they may try to break away in a destructive fashion.

The golden rule for teenagers is to stop talking and start listening. The experts tell us that young people who achieve well academically and have high self-esteem tend to come from families that practise democracy in the home as their teenagers show a growing sense of responsibility.

A psychologist friend tells me that she is convinced that the key with teenagers is to create a win–win situation. It's not 'I'm your parent, so I have to win.' It's 'How can we sort this out?'

Learn to co-operate with your teenagers, and expect the best of them. Then learn to make deals with them.

Unfortunately an adolescent's response to feeling unloved, unaccepted and invalidated is often to rebel against the rules.

- ✪ Notice your teenager's abilities and compliment them.
- ✪ Ask your teenager's opinion on an issue. You will create new levels of respect when you value their perspective. You don't have to agree with it, but you can genuinely listen and try to understand.

○   Work with your teenager to establish realistic
     rules for telephone use, television quotas,
     transport, and allowances.

When there is a battle on, work out a deal. Set fair boundaries, even if you have to compromise your own standards
a bit. As a father, you can often arbitrate. Then, having done
a deal, you will need to monitor how the teenagers keep
their end of the bargain. Some of the areas you may want
to negotiate with your teenagers are:

○   room rules,
○   church attendance,
○   driving licence,
○   tattoos.

Room rules could be:

○   no smelly clothes,
○   no crude posters,
○   nothing on the floor.

This may not suit the parental desire for a tidy house, but
it will be a realistic expectation and should strike the
teenager as fair.

Some suggestions for negotiating on church attendance are:

○   'Perhaps you don't have to come every week, but
     how about you come once a fortnight?'
○   'Mum and I would appreciate your coming with us,
     because we believe the spiritual side of life is
     important.'

✪ 'We are quite happy for you to attend a church where your friends go.'

When it comes to tattoos, or other peer-driven issues, try the following opening remarks.

✪ 'People judge young people with tattoos in a certain way. I don't want that to happen to you.'
✪ 'I wouldn't like you, at fourteen, to make a decision you will later regret. When you are seventeen (or whatever age both parents think appropriate), you can make up your own mind about it.'

Kids and the family car need not be a hassle. Sorting out fair use of the family car once your teenager has a driving licence is where you need to introduce some negotiating skills. Negotiate a contract with your teenager for using the car. Try something along the lines of: 'Now that you are getting your licence, how about you write the rules (or the contract) for using the car.' Your young driver may forget the one about cleaning the car, or filling up the tank, and you can keep negotiating until you feel happy. You may also want to get your child to think about the safety of being on the motorway after a certain time of night, especially after parties begin to shut down.

Believe it or not, conflicts with your children can provide opportunities to grow closer together. Every problem is a "significant life learning situation". When your adolescent child talks about a problem, show empathy and listen, but don't rush in to rescue. Try lines like these for starters:

- ✪ 'That's sad.'
- ✪ 'That's a problem, darling, what's your plan to sort it out?'
- ✪ 'What can you tell me that will reassure me that you will be safe at this party?'
- ✪ 'Give me three reasons why you think this is going to work.'

Social contracts are a good way to negotiate a fair deal with teenagers. Here are some potential areas of conflict where contracts can come in handy:

- ✪ videos,
- ✪ bed making and room tidying,
- ✪ bathroom times, and
- ✪ household chores.

Explain what you mean by the term social contract—that in return for your supplying (or allowing) certain things your teenager wants (use of the family car, a larger allowance etc), the teen agrees to keep the bedroom tidy, make the bed, pack the dishwasher etc. When discussing the terms of the contract, always remember the "atmosphere":

- ✪ Keep it warm and friendly. Be empathic, even slightly nonchalant.
- ✪ Be firm, but keep your voice light.
- ✪ Don't rescue your child. Allow him to own his problem and find a solution.

Finally, I'd like to warn you of the possible outcomes of trying to hold on to unhealthy control over your child in those important years when teenagers are finding their identity and struggling to be seen as trustworthy. During the parenting seminars that I conduct with Mary, we talk about different parenting styles. You may recognise this one and the outcomes.

The parentus sergeant majorcus species. You usually can't recognise this species by the way they look, but you can by the types of noises they make. They make noises like: 'I don't have to give you a reason. Just do it because I'm your father and I say so!'

Recognise the style? Lots of rules and instructions, but very few reasons. Harsh discipline, but not much emotional support. Too many fathers behave like this. Perhaps it's the only style of parenting they saw when they were growing up, or perhaps they have chosen to be this kind of parent because: 'I want my kids to turn out perfectly. I'm going to put so many rules and regulations around them, they won't have a chance to put a foot wrong.'

How do kids with this kind of parent respond, especially when they hit adolescence? They rebel. They might be very well-behaved little children (they had no option but to be), but as teenagers, they really kick over the traces. Why?

- ✪ Because the rules were never presented with reasons, the children never believed that the things that were prohibited by their parents were actually wrong. Instead, they just thought their parents were killjoys.
- ✪ Because they knew that breaking the rules would be severely punished, the children got very good at not being caught—they learnt how to look

good, but still do things behind their parents'
backs.

One final tragedy for the children of the parentus sergeant
majorcus: you can understand them not liking their parents,
but they tend to not even like themselves. They often have
crushingly low self-esteem, probably because they didn't get
any of that praise and affirmation that little kids need as
they grow up. Or perhaps they only ever heard the "try
harder" messages from their parents.

We also identify the parentus jellyfishicus and the parentus
absentus, as sub-groups of parental species, both of whom
leave children with unresolved security and self-control
issues.

A parentus jellyfishicus would say things like:

- ✪ 'Are you in trouble at school again? Those awful
  teachers, they gang up on you, don't they! I'm
  going down to that school to straighten them out.'
- ✪ 'So you want to watch that movie on television
  tonight? It's on awfully late, and I'd hate you to be
  too tired at school tomorrow, dear. So you take
  tomorrow off, and I'll send a note to school saying
  you're not well.'
- ✪ 'Do you mind if I borrow my car from you
  tomorrow? It looks as if it might rain and I'd like
  to do your paper run for you.'

Well, maybe there aren't many parents quite as wet as that,
but parentus jellyfishicus parents are far from uncommon.
Their main characteristic is that they fail to set limits and

boundaries for their kids. You see this type of parent often in supermarkets with their small child thrashing around on the floor, while the parent looks pathetic and says, 'Isn't he a little character? I can't do a thing with him.'

The children of parentus jellifishicus have almost the same self-esteem problems as the children of parentus sergeant majorcus. How come, you might wonder, since these parents are often very liberal in their praise, tending to trickle golden syrup all over their kids: 'You're so clever. You're so beautiful. You're such a good boy.' Why would such children have low self-esteem?

There is a secret to self-esteem: healthy self-esteem doesn't depend on other people; it comes from being able to pat yourself on the back and say, 'No one else might notice. No one else might applaud. But I know I did the right thing. I made the right decision. I am a good person.' The parentus jellifishicus's children never get those gifts, because they never have to reach standards, and they are constantly being rescued—before they feel the pain and before they get the gain. Even little children come to associate a lack of rules and boundaries with a lack of love and caring. And teenagers ultimately despise weak parents who won't stand up to them.

Parentus absentus: One of our modern tragedies is parents who, because of the demands of their careers, have put their children in the care of others. Parents need to know that they are the builders, while all others are merely subcontractors.

There is another type of parent: parentus backbonicus. A backbone is a wonderful thing—all of us should try and have one. They are flexible but strong; they bend so far, but no further. This type of parent sets rules, but they are not like the rules of the parentus sergeant majorcus.

- ✪ The child will always understand why the rules are there.
- ✪ The rules are fair, and the child knows that they are an expression of the parents' love and protection.

These parents don't always say 'No!' Instead, they say, 'Convince me. Give me a reason.' They are open to negotiation. These parents also realise that their children grow up, and that rules need to change with changing times. They know that the rules for a ten-year-old are not appropriate for a fourteen-year-old.

They practise the grandparents' rule: 'You can do what you want to do when you've done what you have to do.'
They are inspirational parents. They have ideas, they plan events and they know the value of delayed gratification. They know that a child needs, and can savour, the experience of saving up for a bike or looking forward to a special treat. They are aware that a child who is given everything he wants immediately is denied the joy of expectation and the process of seeing the savings grow.

The loving and firm parentus backbonicus is creative and open to negotiation. Here's how this type of parent might negotiate a curfew.

When Richard is thirteen, his parents sit him down and ask him, 'How would you like to be setting your own curfew by the time you are sixteen?' He is a bit amazed and says something like 'Cool!' Then his parents make him a simple proposition. His curfew in the weekends is currently 9 pm. If he does not violate that curfew for six months, then it is bumped up to 9:30 pm. Every six violation-free months thereafter, his curfew is moved forward another 30 minutes. When he turns sixteen—given that he has co-operated with the plan, he graduates from an 11:30 pm curfew to setting his own. The only condition is that coming in even one minute late is a violation, and there are no excuses. A violation will cause whatever six-month period he is in to begin anew. That means that when he turns sixteen his curfew could still be 9 pm!

Having understood and agreed on the plan, a parent and teenager can shake hands and a deal is struck. It is a deal which puts control into the teenager's hands and allows him to live up to his parents' trust.

The teenager, if he keeps his side of the bargain, will by age sixteen, be setting his own curfew—letting his parents know when he's leaving the house in the evening and when he will be home. This is both a freedom and a commitment. If he fails to come home when promised, the curfew would revert to 11.30 pm for six months.

It is amazing how even a highly social, outgoing and head-strong young person will rise to the respect that this type of contract gives them, and never, ever come in late.

Daniel Goleman, in his book *Emotional Intelligence*, reports that statistics from several studies show how parents who are involved, and who set consistent guidelines for their children, are rewarded with young adults who have developed a 'set of traits'—some call it character—that matter immensely for their personal destiny.

Remember, rules without reasons create rebellion.
Kids need predictability. They need to know what positive consequences will occur if they work hard, and what discomforts they will have to endure if they slacken off. Parents who are on opposite ends of the spectrum—either over-permissive or irrationally strict—force children to guess at the consequences of their behaviour.

Here are the cardinal rules for discipline (adapted from *Don't Be Afraid to Discipline*, by Dr Ruth Peters):

- Be consistent.
- Take a cool, calm, almost nonchalant attitude.
- Make sure the consequences are immediate, important to the child, predictable and calmly given.
- Rules that lead to consequences should be clear, jointly determined by both parent and child, and fair.

Catch your kids doing something right and praise them. Make sure they don't have to misbehave to get your attention.

A STRATEGY FOR
HELPING YOUR CHILDREN
HANDLE MONEY

*My daughter always has too much month left over
the end of her money.*

Author Unknown

*A little gained honestly is better than great wealth gotten
by dishonest means.*

Proverbs 16:6 (*The Living Bible*)

A Strategy for Helping Your Children Handle Money

⊛ Don't give your children pocket money for doing chores. Children need to learn that certain chores are a necessary part of belonging to a family and taking responsibility for themselves.

⊛ Give your children an amount appropriate to their age.

⊛ Divide the cash into thirds and use three jars to 'bank' the money. The first jar is for saving, the second for spending and the third is the family tax jar! The family tax is used for holidays, outings and money to give to charity. The whole family decides how the family tax is spent.

The way your children value money will have a lot to do with the way they view life. If children understand the link between work and money, and have the experience and excitement of saving for things they want, then they will be well equipped for life.

It is important that children have some money of their own to spend. Children may become manipulative if they always have to ask you for everything. Allow them the joy of choosing to save rather than spend, or spending on something they really want, but that you might consider frivolous. Children only learn through experience. It is better for them to practise husbanding money and learn the realities of frittering it away instead of saving it.

Decide on an amount of pocket money for each child according to their age and set up your own system. Use the jar method from the strategy box to help them connect with the idea of allocating their funds.

A family I know gives their children pocket money on Friday nights in little brown envelopes, similar to the old wage packet. Each has the following note:
'With love from Mum and Dad.

Save some, spend some and give some!
By the way, we had to dock 50 cents because your bed wasn't made on Tuesday.'

If your child is saving for something special, you may like to draw up a chart so that he or she can see progress towards the goal—a thermometer, or some other visual symbol, will do the job. You might like to pay the child for extra jobs done, or occasionally for good marks or willing behaviour. In this way you can all enjoy the experience of working towards the savings goal.

Remember, children tend to have a poor sense of the future. Don't gratify every whim and desire. If you do, you will rob your children of the joy of expectation and the satisfaction of knowing that they earned the new bike, computer, video game etc.

They also learn that everyday necessities have to be paid for by someone.

If your teenagers resent you buying their clothes and want to take control of their clothing allowance, allow them to do so. Give them the money you would normally spend on their clothes for a year.

Remember the boundaries; as long as something is not physically harmful or morally harmful, let your children make their own mistakes. A teenager may spend his whole allowance on a cap with a bend in it and a pair of Doc Martins—that is OK. You can merely empathise, and reaffirm your belief in his ability to think of ways to clothe himself for the rest of the time. If he blows the money, don't belittle him. Just say: 'That's a bit of a 'shocker', but you're a smart kid; you'll work something out.' And he will. Don't rescue him. He will discover second-hand clothing shops. He may even learn to sew!

It will be this kind of experience that will imprint the need to budget more carefully next time.

When on holiday, a good plan is to give your children a daily allowance. This lets them buy their own ice-creams or odd indulgences, and will stop them begging you for treats.

A Strategy for Having Fun

*A cheerful heart is good medicine, but a crushed spirit
dries up the bones.*

Proverbs 17:22 (*The Living Bible*)

*A father is soneone who will play with you, even though he has
friends his own age to play with.*

6-year-old

A STRATEGY FOR HAVING FUN

Dads do the kid-fun stuff well—or they like to think they do. Learn to switch into 'fun-mode' whenever possible.

✪ Suggest picnics and outings. Don't let pressure squeeze out the spontaneous from your life.

✪ Turn jobs into fun. Dance and sing and act parts.

✪ Rock 'n' roll with your kids. Let them lip-synch using a banana as a microphone as you conduct with a spoon.

✪ Be playful with your spouse. Pinches, tickles or a long mushy kiss in front of your kids will guarantee a few giggles.

In my experience in dealing with families in crisis, very often the real problem is the atmosphere. Children remember very few of the day-to-day details of their childhoods, but they always remember how it felt— the atmosphere. In some families, there is just something in the air.

Fun creates the right atmosphere. Fun builds communication. Fun builds relationships.

Parents may be doing many things right with their children, but if the atmosphere is terrible, your children will not feel free to become who they were meant to be. Parents might be saying wonderful things to their teenager, but if he senses disapproval in their tone or body language, then he is likely to switch on the silent treatment and lock his parents right out of his world. (My other book, *The Whitewater Rafting Years: A Commonsense Guide to Parenting Teenagers*, has some sections on the silent treatment, and other such hassles.)

Fun also builds a sense of humour. Your children will probably be alarmed, in years to come, to find themselves telling the same jokes and silly stories that they groan at now when you tell them. So switch into "fun-mode" whenever possible and treat yourself to a dose of healthy, stress-reducing endorphins.

You don't have to be a comedian to be a fun father. You just have to appreciate the importance of fun as a major ingredient in a successful family.

One of the best ways to have fun with your kids is getting down to their level. Spend time on the floor wrestling, playing their games, being involved in what they are doing—their toys, their ideas of fun.

Introduce surprise and spontaneity. Do something crazy together on the spur of the moment! Just for fun, pick up your children in their pyjamas, when you arrive home late one night, and take them for a jaunt. Perhaps drive in to a Take-away for a milkshake, or drive around the streets to see the Christmas lights. Your kids will ask why you did that and you can just reply, 'Because you're the best and you're in my team!'

Try some of these:

- a wardrobe full of balloons on their birthday,
- a decorated bedroom as a surprise,
- an Easter egg hunt,
- sleeping in a tent in the backyard,
- sleeping on mattresses in front of the fire,
- telling creepy children's stories in the dark,
- family car cleaning plus sponge wars with buckets of soapy water and sponges,
- popping popcorn, or
- celebrating any special occasion that you care to invent.

Planning a scavenger hunt or a jungle safari is great fun for little ones. Distribute all their soft animal toys around the house. Turn off the lights. Give each child a torch. They are allowed to switch it on for two seconds and see how many animals they can shoot with the torch beam. Keep scores and have fun prizes. This may seem a lot of effort, but ten minutes of organising will create lifetime memories.

Play board games and computer games. Playing together is a great way of teaching about sportsmanship, taking turns, winning and losing graciously, honesty and fairness.

However, even during the fun times, it is still important that you remain the adult. Sometimes when men get involved in games, they become competitive, and forget that the child is smaller, may be tired at the end of a day, and may just need cuddles and quiet stories, rather than chasing and wrestling.

So, dads, stay in charge. It's your job to see that no one gets hurt, that everyone plays fair and has fun. Don't send a child out of the game forever. If a child isn't coping or playing within the rules, don't send the child away with the message that they are a wimp or a bad sport. Call a five-minute break. Give the child some breathing space. Let the child join in again, or watch the others, or go and do something else.

Make sure you finish a game while everyone is still having fun. Your fun won't be fun any more if the games always finish in tears and shouting. If you see that trouble is brewing, finish the game and go and celebrate with a snack or a drink.

You can also use fun as a way to make a point. Learn to hassle your kids back when they are hassling you. Keep a light tone in your voice, and when your child asks to be let off a block before school so as not to be embarrassed by being seen with you, cordially agree. However, next time you go to the Mall with him, ask politely if he will get out a block or two before you reach the shops, so that none of your friends see you with him!

Sick of being grunted at by your teenager? Assume that it means something! For instance, after school, try to establish a meaningful dialogue:
'How did your day go? What did you learn?'
'Ungph … umf!'
'Really? You learnt the same thing yesterday!'
Turning a situation to humour might not help their sanity, but it will preserve the last shreds of yours.

Don't neglect to cultivate the fun and romance in your marriage. Kids need fathers who love their mothers. Plan surprises. Dress up in your best suit on your wedding anniversary and let your children dress up in their favourite clothes as the bridesmaids and best man. Repeat your wedding vows and then dance by candle-light in the lounge afterwards. (Our children loved this.) If you don't realise that having fun together is one of the healthiest things you can do for your relationship, then you really are a boring old toad. Shape up, before someone ships out, from sheer boredom.

Let your children see extravagant and fun demonstrations of affection. Let them:

✪   help you choose or make a card for your wife,
✪   carry flowers in from the car (but make sure that
       they know that the flowers are your gift to your
       wife, not theirs),
✪   see you hug and cuddle,

Sometimes teenagers will pretend to throw up when parents do mushy stuff. They have to react like that, because they're teenagers (mocking parents is part of their job description), but secretly, it is reassuring. 'Isn't it great that Dad is still madly keen on Mum ... but I'm sure he doesn't know how to make love!'

That atmosphere of fun will be a powerful example for your children's future relationships.

A STRATEGY FOR KEEPING YOUR CHILDREN SAFE FROM PREDATORS

People in this country demonstrate that a person is considered more evil if he steals money from adults than if he steals innocence from children.

Deborah Coddington, 'The Sex Offenders Index'

A STRATEGY FOR KEEPING YOUR CHILDREN SAFE FROM PREDATORS

- ✪ When you are dressing a child in their swimsuit, it is a very natural thing to explain, as matter-of-factly as possible, that whatever area their swimsuit covers is where no one should touch them. 'It is OK for the doctor, if Mum or Dad is there.'

- ✪ Explain that if they don't feel OK about something that an adult does, they can say, 'I don't like that' and always tell you.

- ✪ Be aware of the importance of not having "secrets" in the family—have surprises instead.

- ✪ Ask them, without making a big deal of it, what they would do if someone tried to touch them inappropriately.

- ✪ Give your children a family password. Explain that they only go with people who know the password. So if anyone stops them and says, 'Your mother told me to pick you up', they'll know never to go unless the person knows the password. (Explain obvious exceptions such as the police.) Practise what they would do if a stranger asked them to go with him or her, without knowing the password.

- ✪ Fathers should be aware of the kinds of places that paedophiles hang around in—children's playgrounds, sports grounds, beaches.

- ✪ Be aware that most children who are abused by adults are abused by people they already know.

Although we want to protect our young children by not exposing them to unnecessary fears, it is a sad fact that there are paedophiles in our community. It is also a sad fact that many children have suffered child abuse in their own home or classroom.

Child pornography and mental illness have, in the past, been responsible for behaviour leading to children being abducted, abused and sometimes murdered. Our children will have the least chance of this happening to them if they are living in a stable home where both parents are vigilant and on deck. Paedophiles will often take a lot of time working on their young victims, orchestrating an emotional dependence and trust, before they actually move on the child. They will often instinctively pick on children who are deprived in some way and use the lure of presents, lollies or outings to ingratiate themselves with the children and, occasionally, their families.

Paedophiles will also use violence and fear: 'This is our secret, and something terrible will happen to your Mummy and Daddy if you tell' or 'Don't tell anyone, or I'll kill your whole family.'

However, there are also opportunistic situations when young children are abducted and abused. It always amazes me, when one of these cases is reported, how many known child abusers the police can identify as living in any particular area. For this reason, we must make sure that our children are able to protect themselves and, without destroying their innocence or making them afraid to venture out or ever to use a public toilet, ensure they know what to do if they find themselves in danger.

At a course I attended at Denver University in 1998, I talked to a woman police officer who has specialised in this sort of crime. She explained how in one particularly sad situation, a family was watching their young son playing soccer. Their three-year-old daughter wanted to go to the toilet. The parents saw it was only a short distance off and let her go on her own. She was later found murdered and abused in the toilet. The police asked for parents who had attended the match with video cameras to hand in any footage that they had, in order to check out the crowd. The police were astonished to identify six known paedophiles on the sidelines of the school soccer match, including the referee.

Her advice to parents was to make sure that children know they can tell their parents everything, and allow times in your day when a child feels safe to communicate (the end-of-the-bed talks—the nicest thing that happened today, the yukkiest thing that happened).

Make sure you always know where your children are. Make sure they never walk to and from school alone and check on them after sports practice etc.

Make sure that windows in children's bedrooms are securely fastened and that you sleep close enough to your children's rooms to hear them and respond if they need you in the night.

If you feel uneasy about a certain individual around your child, you can ring the sex-offenders section of your local police.

Give your children a family password and make sure that they know that they are never to accompany anyone home in a car, unless that person has been given the password by you.

An eight-year-old boy from Christchurch, New Zealand, was interviewed on a current affairs program earlier this year. The story explained how a paedophile had tried to coax him to come in the car, claiming that the boy's mother had sent him to collect the child from school. Because the driver did not know the family password, this little guy refused to go with him. The interviewer, Paul Holmes, praised the kid for his level-headedness and, at the end of the interview, leaned towards him conspiratorially and asked, 'So what was the password?' The boy said, 'I'm not going to tell you!'

That was a well-coached boy! His parents had practised the scenario with him, and he was prepared when an adult did try to catch him off guard.

In the USA, since the introduction of 'Megan's Law', 49 States have laws which enforce registration of convicted paedophiles. Here's how Megan's Law happened.

Megan Kanka, a seven-year-old from New Jersey, was kidnapped, raped and murdered in 1993 by a twice-convicted child molester who lived nearby. After her parents and others fought for tougher notification laws, Megan's Law was passed. It means that when paedophiles and rapists are freed from jail, and move into their communities, local officials must be supplied with information about them. On the day the law was signed President Clinton said:

'We respect people's rights, but today America proclaims there is no greater right than a parent's right to raise a child in safety and love... America warns—if you dare to prey on our children, the law will follow you wherever you go, State to State, town to town.'

Parents need to be active in protecting children and in lobbying for a law similar to that passed by the US Congress.

Children spend a lot of time on the Internet these days. It is full of useful resources and information for their schoolwork and projects—and just for interest and fun. It is also an area in which you will need to establish family rules that keep your children safe from predators.

A good rule is to explain to your family that the same principles apply for leaving the safe and known sites, as would for going down a dark street at night on your own. Don't go to sites that are not known without an adult there.

Keep your family computer in a room where you can keep an eye on what your children are doing. Even if you are not computer literate yourself, you can still monitor what your children are doing.

Set up (or make sure your children set up) the facility on the toolbar of your computer for their favourite web sites, or bookmark them. Explain to young children that those are the sites that they can access on their own. Spend time adding new sites to their favourites list.

Be vigilant whenever the Internet is involved. Unscrupulous people continually place obscene and pornographic material on the Internet under innocent-sounding names.

Be aware that some electronic games are becoming more violent; some have particularly "dark" themes. Sit down with your child and play each of the games that your child acquires with him/her to reassure yourself that they are suitable.

A STRATEGY FOR ADDRESSING ANGER

If you are patient in one moment of anger, you will escape a hundred days of sorrow.

Chinese Proverb

Anger blows out the lamp of the mind.

Robert Green Ingersoll

A STRATEGY FOR ADDRESSING ANGER

✪ Stay calm when your child is upset.

✪ Accept and acknowledge your child's feelings, and help your child verbalise them.

✪ Allow cooling-off time.

✪ Address the cause of the anger.

✪ Talk to your child about the choices we have when we feel angry. These three behaviour skills are vital for the rest of their lives:
walk away until you have calmed down,
think about whether it matters or not, and
remind yourself that it is OK if things don't always go your way; you can handle it.

✪ Explain to your child the anger rules. It's OK to feel angry, but:
don't hurt others,
don't hurt yourself,
don't hurt things, and
do talk about it

✪ Talking about the anger can be like allowing the steam to escape, but rehearsing and reliving the anger may establish negative patterns that stay with you for life.

Anger is a universal emotion. It is also misunderstood. Unfortunately, adults often pass on to children unhealthy patterns of dealing with anger.

My relationship with my father, during my childhood, oscillated between his treating me with great kindness, and then with bouts of often unexplained frustration and unpredictable anger. It left me confused.

One of the earliest memories I have of my father was when I was four years old. He was working for a timber company, driving timber trucks between Wellington and Levin. I was promised a whole day riding in the cab of the truck on his next delivery run. My life was on hold as I anticipated this "men's day out". I packed my tool box and my builder's apron. Mum packed me a lunch in a box like Dad's, and I set off for what I remember as the adventure of a lifetime. I was just four, but just for a day, I was a man amongst men. The other timber workers treated me with great dignity and kindness, and they called me 'Bill', the name that I insisted Mum call me, when I was "building" things at home! All up, it was a great day with my Dad.

I also have a vivid memory of the time he came home to

find me playing in the shed with his tools. He was furious and dispatched me from his shed with a thorough and painful spanking. His anger, as well as the injustice of the situation, left me confused and upset. I wanted to be like Dad. I loved building things and I loved tools. But Dad excluded me from the thing I longed to do—work at things with tools, just like he did—and it crushed me. I wasn't given an opportunity to put things right, to make up for what I had done, or to learn from the situation. I was the butt of his frustration and anger. By dinnertime, my father was back to his normal, jolly self. But I wasn't. The event was not mentioned again.

When I was seventeen, my father bought his first new car. He refused to teach me how to drive. This car was his pride and joy, and the unspoken message was that I couldn't be trusted with it. At nineteen I went to a driving school to get my licence, but I was never allowed to use the family car. The first occasion on which Mum managed to talk him into lending it to me, was for a 200-kilometre trip I needed to make to a nearby town, where I was scheduled to run a youth program. Unfortunately, driving home late the next evening I fell asleep at the wheel, hit a pile of shingle and rolled his precious new car!

It cost me a lot of money, but the greater cost was enduring my father's anger. He didn't speak to me for three weeks. His silence yelled at me, 'All my lack of trust in you was justified!'

I don't recall these memories in order to discredit my father. He was a loving, caring man and I know that his anger embarrassed him. However, he was a man of his time and his own upbringing, a man who seldom talked about his feelings. Things like examining emotions were just put in the too-hard basket.

I admired my father's integrity and work ethic, and the stable home he provided for me. I also admired the practical kind-heartedness he showed to neighbours and the young people from the youth groups he ran. He also, in later years, became a kindly and much-loved Grandad.

However, I grew into adulthood with few tools to deal with my own frustration and anger. I have had to learn to try to deal with my anger, to process frustration and to work on breaking the "generational cycle".

I now hope that my boys have some of the life skills and the insights that they need, in order to ensure that they will not give their wives the hard time I sometimes gave Mary.

I have learnt that I have choices about my own reactions. That I can choose to escalate my anger or to trace the reason for my anger and make a choice about how I will act.

The five things that have helped me are:

- ✪ Does it really matter? Why start World War III over the milk being left out of the refrigerator, or the mud patches on my newly sown lawn from the children's cricket games?
- ✪ What are you telling yourself? Get healthy messages in your head rather than 'No one listens to me' or 'I have a right to get angry.'
- ✪ Count to ten before you say anything. A slow

response is a thought-out one—and it gives you time to cool it.

◉ Express what needs to happen without getting angry. Be assertive without bulldozing other people.

◉ It's OK if things go wrong. They can be fixed.

An excellent question to ask yourself is: 'Does this child's action deserve my reaction?' This will give you a clue as to whether the anger is something about you (for instance an overreaction from your past), rather than an appropriate response to your child's behaviour.

Remember, if parents violate a child's sense of justice by not listening to their genuine concerns as well as not listening to what's behind their frustration, then they put the child on the stuck-in-an-emotional-pattern track. The child is more likely to use anger as a kind of self-defence against not being understood.

Show you are really listening with comments or questions that will open communication:

◉ 'You look frustrated.'
◉ 'Come and tell me what is upsetting you.'
◉ 'Can you tell me what's wrong?'
◉ 'Anything else?'

Good self-esteem means less need for anger. Listening to our children and believing in them will dissipate much anger. Seeing them as kind, generous, loving and hardworking will help them to grow into those sorts of people. Let go of always trying to control them or trying to "fix" them. Love your children unconditionally and show it!

Make sure that you have listening times and times of focused attention established in your home.

Have a family gripe meeting where grievances can be aired and solutions sorted out.

If a child has been wronged, acknowledge that people shouldn't have treated the child that way and accept his feelings of anger. Then explain that he has a choice about his reaction to what happened.

You can help your child interpret what is going on by explaining that when other people treat him badly, for no reason, it is that other person's problem, not your child's.

Help your children to use humour to defuse an angry situation, and to walk away.

TEACH YOUR CHILD THE ANGER RULES

Have a family rule for cooling down. It may be that you just quietly and firmly hold a panicky young child while he or she settles down, or you may use another tried and true idea—the child goes to his or her room until he or she cools down. Even to run around the block or kick a ball around the backyard can give the physical adrenaline rush (prompted by anger) time to fade.

In her excellent book, *Anger! The Misunderstood Emotion*, Dr Carol Travis makes some interesting observations. After a careful and very thorough review of the anger literature, she concludes that freely venting anger doesn't relieve the anger; it actually increases it. Letting yourself rant and rave can truly be harmful to your health. But the really dangerous aspect of anger, she points out, is not stifling it, but feeling it in the first place. If you act out your anger, you reinforce it. Eventually you may establish a hostile habit. It is better, Travis argues, to 'keep quiet about your momentary irritations and distract yourself with pleasant activity until your fury simmers down'. Chances are that you will feel better, and feel better faster, that way than if you let yourself go.

Children often need leadership from us and the security that a firm father gives in setting boundaries. Their father's presence in the home will be a modifying influence on children's behaviour, especially if he can learn the skill of setting boundaries on his own anger, as well as his child's:

- Helping children make choices about anger is part of the values equation.
- Helping children understand about healthy personal boundaries shows them that repaying meanness with kindness is part of that golden rule: 'Do to others what you would like them to do to you.' They will learn from this universal principle that when we treat other people well, that courtesy is likely to be reflected back.
- Letting children know that the qualities of patience, contentedness, self-denial and generosity are valued, puts in place one of the cornerstones of character.
- Teach your children the proverb 'It is better to be slow-tempered than famous; it is better to have self-control than to control an army.' (Proverbs 16:32)

Remember, anger is a signal. You are allowed to be outraged if someone harms your child in any way. Your children are relying on you to protect them, and your response shows them that you care. Use your anger to motivate you to do something about the situation. If it is abuse of any kind—bullying, some sort of humiliation, or people wanting to push drugs or pornography on to your kids—don't look the other way. Fight for your children.

However, don't overlook the fact that siblings can also cause a lot of damage to each other. Be the firm but fair dad who refuses to allow children to destroy each other.

Remember:

- ✪ Bad anger destroys good things—marriages and child/father relationships.
- ✪ Good anger destroys bad things—bullies, paedophiles or drug pushers who will abuse children.

A STRATEGY FOR AVOIDING FOOD FADDINESS

A gourmet can tell from the flavour whether a woodcock's leg is the one on which the bird is accustomed to roost.

Lucius Beebe

A STRATEGY FOR
AVOIDING FOOD FADDINESS

Try the 'Dad's Deal' approach:

✪ Suggest that you are going to give the family an amnesty on three foods each, for a whole month. Allow each child to write down three foods that they don't want to have to eat this month. These become their amnesty foods. They don't have to eat their amnesty foods for a whole month. But they do have to eat everything else without complaining—that's the deal.

✪ Buy a low, flat, plastic container with a lid for each child. Get the children to decorate their lids with their own name, picture etc. Explain that anything that is left on a child's plate will go into their container, and if they become hungry between meals, then they can look in the fridge to see what is their container!

✪ Have a family night, once a week, and let the children take turns at being in charge. They can choose the menu for their family night as well as a game or activity. They can learn to help cook their favourite meal. If each child learns a specialty, such as Sam's Special Salad or Fiona's Fettuccine, they are less likely to refuse to eat it.

✪ Don't fight over food. If a child senses that eating is important to you, you may end up with a power struggle on your hands.

✪ Model good table manners at all times if you want your children to have good table manners.

I still eat beetroot at a smorgasbord dinner because my mother told me that it would keep my blood red! Many children have discovered, at some point in their young lives, that parents will try many and devious strategies to get junior to eat. We will tell them stories about starving children that don't have any food. We play aeroplanes—trying to trick them to swallow a mouthful before they notice—or we present masses of different foods, hoping to tempt them to eat something and so "make Mum and Dad happy".

When a child realises that his eating is very important to parents, he suddenly has a really useful weapon.

How many family stories revolve around food that you hated? Children who went to boarding school remember the meals—often the same each week—with fond repulsion. I have never eaten macaroni cheese since I worked on a radio station where we had macaroni cheese every Thursday night. These stories are part of family folklore, but too often, food wars become a very serious dynamic in a family, and cause great harm later on. A child who learns to use food as a way of controlling parents may later use food as a way of keeping control over other areas of her life for the wrong reasons. It is vital that we don't allow food

233

to become too important when children are small.

Fathers can be good and objective umpires in the food faddiness wars. Just a firm rule—that you have to try a little bit of everything—is sometimes enough. A child will sometimes try to refuse his mother, when just a firm instruction from father is enough to ensure he gobbles it down.

Let your children take responsibility for their own level of hunger. Here are two strategies:

- ✪ When meals aren't eaten, don't rescue your child. Merely empathise that your child has the problem (there is no more food until breakfast). Say something like 'That's a shame, but breakfast is in twelve hours!'
- ✪ Hand around the serving dish of vegetables rather than serving the vegetables on the plate for the child. It is amazing what children will eat when they are allowed to choose what and how much for themselves.

A STRATEGY FOR
HANDLING SWEARING, SPITTING
AND OTHER OFF-LIMITS STUFF!

When I was:
4 years old: My daddy could do anything.
6 years old: My dad is smarter than your dad.
14 years old: Don't pay any attention to my father. He is so
old-fashioned.
30 years old: Maybe we should ask Dad what he thinks.
After all he's had a lot of experience.
50 years old: I'd give anything if Dad were here now,
so I could talk this over with him.

Ann Landers

A Strategy for Handling Swearing, Spitting and Other Off-limits Stuff!

✪ Explain what certain swearwords mean and why, as a family, you don't want anyone to use those words.

✪ Explain the significance of the labels other people put on you, when you speak in a certain way.

✪ Set a firm boundary on crude and disrespectful language.

✪ Use a monitoring system such as a swearing fine jar.

✪ Help your children think of appropriate words they can use when they are really frustrated such as 'goodnight', 'sugar', 'stink' etc.

✪ Take your boys or girls out occasionally and allow them to do some (harmless) normally 'off-limits' stuff.

At one of our Hot Tips for Parents seminars, a father approached me at morning tea. He thanked me for the advice I had given him three years ago and wanted to share the outcome. He told me how a few years ago, when he had just been released from prison, his little boy of three had begun spitting. He had belted his son, because that was all he knew to do. Concerned neighbours had paid for him to come to one of our seminars, where he asked me, 'How do you stop a three-year-old spitting?'

No one had ever asked me that one before, so I suggested he challenge his young son to a spitting competition every night, to see who was the best spitter. However, part of the "competition" was that he also solemnly shook hands with his little boy at the end of the session each night, and told him that, as this was men's stuff, he was not to spit at any other time!

I remember my wife Mary nearly dying on the plane home when I told her what I had said!

A year or so later, after a follow-up evening, the man approached me again and said, 'My little boy loved the spitting contest. It was a great bonding exercise because it was our men's thing each night.' He then went on to explain that after a week or so, his youngster had tired of it, and that ended the whole episode of spitting for attention. The rewarding outcome for me was that the father by now was so enthusiastic about the success of the "spitting contest" that he started talking about parenting at work. He showed me his dog-eared parenting manual and said, 'My mates and I talk parenting every Wednesday at lunchtime at the factory.'

Kids will often pick up a swearword and be fascinated by it. Here's a strategy that may release the pressure of the fascination with a swearword. Try saying something like:
'It seems like you like the sound of that word. It seems you feel you need to say it. Well, I didn't realise it meant so much to you. In that case you need to say it, but not here in front of us. So you may go into your room and say it a hundred times.'

Point out to the child that only a person with a small vocabulary needs to swear. It's smarter not to swear. There are other ways to ease frustration.

Also explain to your children that what comes out of our mouths is who we are, and using crude words means that that is what you are owning. Give them some harmless words they can use if they are really frustrated. But also explain that their self-talk can help ease their frustration. Get them to tell themselves that:

- ✪ nothing bad will happen if they don't do it right the first time,
- ✪ they don't always have to win to be happy, and
- ✪ they can try again and do it better next time.

When I was seven years old, my mum caught me playing with matches behind the wood shed. She suggested that if I liked playing with matches so much she would watch while I lit a whole box, one at a time, over the incinerator. She then insisted that anytime she needed a fire, I should light it. She would call me in from playing, interrupt my television . . . whenever she needed a fire lit, she called on me. In the end I remember saying to her, 'Can't you light your own fires?'

Rather than always saying 'no', sometimes allowing the out-of-bounds stuff under your supervision can be the right thing to do.

A Strategy for
Dads Who Are Not
Living with Their Children

*Once you have established the goals that you want and the
price you're willing to pay, you can ignore the minor hurts, the
opponent's pressure and temporary failures.*

Vince Lombardi, Coach, Green Bay Packers

A STRATEGY FOR DADS WHO ARE NOT LIVING WITH THEIR CHILDREN

✪ Try to keep amicable relations with your children's mother. Always speak respectfully about her in front of the children.

✪ Write to your children every birthday and Christmas. Tell them what you appreciate about them and your dreams for them. Tell them a funny story and the thing that you most enjoyed doing with them this year.

✪ Try to spend some time when your children are with you, at home, doing chores as well as having fun. Even helping make a bed together with your sons can turn into a good-natured battle with the pillows. It will show your children that being with Dad is not just fun; you also expect them to take some responsibility for jobs.

✪ Always keep a promise. Try to always keep your word when you have promised you will pick up or drop off your children.

✪ Set up some 'Dad's rules', so that the children know where the boundaries are when they are with you.

✪ Keep the lines of communication open by asking them what they think, rather than just what they did.

✪ Make it easy for your children to stay in touch with you when they are not with you.

✪ When things go wrong, try to use a "no-blame" phrase such as, 'This isn't working. How can we work it out in a way that we can all live with?'

Although it is hard to be separated from your children, you can decide to make the most of the time that you do have with them and be the best father you can be during that time.

Remember, you will always be a significant influence in your children's lives, so try to keep the relationship going even if you don't have regular access to your children. Along with their mother, you are their primary relative, and they will always come looking for a relationship with you, even if it is years later.

Children are good observers, but poor interpreters, so they may not always interpret events correctly. They may even be hostile towards you at different times, but if you remain consistent and fair, and make sure that you keep regular contact, you have a chance to minimise the emotional distance between you. Keeping the door open to the possibility of reconnecting in a positive way later, will mean that when your sons or daughters need your emotional support or fatherly wisdom, they can get it with their dignity still intact.

An acquaintance tells how his daughter went into 'the longest sulk in the world,' as he put it. It lasted for nearly six years after his marriage broke up; she saw him as the one who had ruined her life, the one who was responsible for the break-up. As she headed into her teenage years, though, she began to thaw, and with the help of two young step-sisters, began to reconnect and become friends with her father again.

If a child has cut himself off emotionally from you, it is really important that you do everything you can to try to reconnect. You are the adult, and you have to try to understand their pain. You could try gently asking a child this sort of question: 'When were you first offended?' The child may tell you that it is entirely your fault that he or she is growing up in a separated family, or something similar. If you can acknowledge the child's pain and apologise, saying that you are truly sorry for the pain the break-up has caused, you may find that your empathy and acknowledgement are the keys; your humility may unlock a child's closed spirit.

Eventually children grow up, and they begin to understand that even though things may have been tough for you, you were still kind, consistent and available.

If you are separated from your spouse and have suffered emotional hurt through divorce, try not to let resentment— about the property settlement or who got the kids, for instance—poison your life. Unfortunately, resentment is like a blocked shotgun: it hurts the firer more than the person it is aimed at. Try to establish some perspective on your failed relationship, perhaps with the help of a counsellor or a close friend, and become the leader and mentor that your children need. Not living with your children will always be more complicated for you than living with them, but it does mean that the times you have together can be used in a resourceful way.

It is really important to close the authority gap between your ex-spouse and yourself. Children will focus in on any differences in standards, so try to agree with your ex-partner on basic rules in order to avoid confusion for your children. Don't criticise the children's mother, even if she has been less than honourable. A close friend of mine said that when he was growing up his mother was an alcoholic and was really delinquent in the way she treated the children. The irony of the situation, though, was that they hated their father more, because he was always criticising her. Children desperately want to be loyal to both their parents, so try to keep conflict, if it arises, impersonal. Try to look at situations as 'not working' and needing a solution, rather than as being your ex-partner's fault.

If there is conflict with an ex-partner or spouse, try to avoid arguments, scenes and fights when your children are present. And don't use your child as a messenger between you. Communicate directly with the other parent. Equally, if your child is angry at the other parent, don't add fuel to the fire. Encourage your child to talk with the other parent about it.

Keep the children's mother informed about where you are going to be with the children. If she feels she is always kept informed, she is more likely to be relaxed about their being with you.

Try to put some of the ideas in the other chapters of this book into practice. Remember, your children will be looking forward to the times that you are taking them away or picking them up for a visit.

A separated mother asked to see me after a parenting seminar as she was concerned about the anger and sadness in her youngest son. She said it seemed to be related to the fact that his father would promise he was going to take him out, then cancel at the last minute. I suggested that she sit at the end of her son's bed and encourage him to talk about how he felt, or think about a picture that expressed his feelings of being let down.

Remember, it is sometimes important to get the bad feelings out before you (or your children) can start letting the good feelings in. The mother rang me a few days later. She had been astounded by what the little boy said. He said, 'Mum, it is like I am waiting on the station and looking forward to Dad coming on the train to pick me up. But then it is like the train comes along and instead of getting off to get me, Dad just stays on the train and waves to me and I get left on the platform!' What an insightful little boy! You will retain high stocks with your kids if you don't let them down.

Finally, give your child permission to continue a loving relationship with you both, and don't share adult emotional burdens with your children. Maintain your own friendships and keep those issues for your adult friends and allow your children to be children.

The communicating of a man's self to his friend works two contrary effects; for it redoubleth joys, and cutteth griefs in half. For there is no man that imparteth his joys to his friend, but he joyeth the more, and no man that imparteth his griefs to his friend, but he grieveth the less.
(Francis Bacon, 1893.)

LEAVING
A LEGACY

The main ingredient of good leadership is good character.
This is because leadership involves conduct, and conduct is
determined by values. You may call these values by many
names. 'Ethics', 'morality and 'integrity' come to mind, but this
much is clear: Values are what make us who we are.

General Norman Schwarzkopf

M y parents taught me never to take something out without putting something back.
(President George Bush)

The most important letter of the alphabet is 'L'. Because it reminds you to listen, learn and love.
(Mother of an Auckland taxi driver)

Eat a live frog first thing in the morning and nothing worse can happen to you the rest of the day!

How do people dream up such wonderful advice? How about this one:
'If you love something, set it free.
If it returns, you haven't lost it.
If it disappears and never comes back,
Then it wasn't truly yours to begin with.
And if it just sits there watching television,
Unaware that it's been set free,
You're probably married to it.'

It's so easy today to waste time frumping in front of the television; to come home, tuckered out by the day's hard work, and eat dinner in front of the box.

249

But our generation needs fathers as never before. I began this book with the suggestion that your greatest investment in your own future as well as in your children's, will be the values, boundaries and challenges you and your wife or partner set for your family.

What sort of people do you hope that your children will become? Do you want them to grow into young men and women who will contribute? Or are you happy for them to become merely "takers"—people for whom self-absorption is the bottom line?

You will have to put the energy in now if you want to train your children's consciences and give them the best chance of reaching their potential.

Like the successful changeover of the baton in a relay race, the legacies you pass on to your children will have a major impact on their life-races, as well as on those of your grandchildren.

If we make the effort to do it, we certainly won't be looked on, in our old age, as the boring old buzzards that nobody wants to have around.
It's a smart father who takes his mentoring role, along with his inspirational role, seriously.

A friend of mine tells the story of how his ten-year-old decided that she wanted to run in the school cross-country race. He said, 'I adore my daughter, but to be perfectly honest, she is not a natural athlete. She has long gangly legs, and is just is not built for running. However, I agreed that if she really wanted to win the cross-country, I would run with her every evening after work.' The first evening, he came home to find his daughter sitting on the couch in her dressing gown. He asked why, and she replied that the weather was a bit wet and she wasn't feeling very well. He gave her a short talk about the need to make up your mind if you want something and then go for it; that dreams become reality when we become what we want to be, and put in the work. From then on, each night they ran together. Within a few weeks she was running like a professional, and after three months, he had the fun of cheering her on from the sidelines as she won the school cross-country race for her age group!

He said it was amazing—almost scary—how once his daughter saw herself as a runner, she grew into her dream!

Dads, we can coach our children into their potential, but also into their future contribution to society. You have the chance of a daily "team talk" with your kids.

There is no doubt that for all of us, our decisions really do determine our destiny!

Teach your children that the future is not a scary thing, but it is their friend, and that the choices they make will affect their future positively or negatively.

The most important choice they will ever make is what ethic they will live by. You have the chance to take the lead and model the manly character and values you wish to see in them. Our values, from how we spend our money to how we relate to others, will be influenced by what we believe.

Be authentic. Don't ever allow yourself to make excuses as to why you believe one way and act another. In my experience, children will forgive most of the sins of their parents, but they will almost always choke on blatant hypocrisy. Try to parent with grace. You don't have to be perfect, but you do have to admit wrongs and ask for forgiveness.

Set positive expectations for yourself and your children. I once asked our teenagers what factor had most influenced their behaviour during their teenage years. Here's what they said:

'You trusted us and you just expected the best of us. You expected us to do the right thing, but most importantly, you never expected us to do the wrong thing. Many of our friends' parents were always suspicious of them, and were constantly giving the impression that they were afraid their teenagers might be deceiving them in some way. So our friends would say to themselves, "Well if that's what Dad thinks of me, then that's fine, that's how I will act!"'

Encourage service! Young people were made for challenges. It is the idealism of young people, the possibilities of their young lives, and their capacity for dreaming about making the world a better place, that have made my many years in youth work so rewarding.

In the 34 years I have spent in youth work, I worked with teams of thousands of young people, led by slightly older volunteer leaders. These young people put together professional-standard concerts, packing both the Wellington and Auckland Town Halls on Saturday nights. They ran youth clubs and organised large social events for teenagers. I was amazed at the level of commitment and energy that teenagers were prepared to give, in order to make something happen. My own children were involved in Campus Life Clubs and I am grateful for the other leaders that influenced their lives.

There is no doubt in my mind that happiness is a by-product of serving. Teenagers' greatest needs are for:

- ✪ social connection with a group,
- ✪ mentoring by healthy men and women outside the family, and
- ✪ lots of physical and mental challenges dished up with a healthy cocktail of fun.

All these needs are naturally met in the camaraderie of club leadership. Look for positive peer groups that will challenge their leadership and willingness to serve.

Finally, never lose the wonder of what it means to be a dad. Professor Francis Collins, who is overseeing the Human Genome Project (a project to map all the genes in the human body) in the USA, was talking in a television interview about the greatness of the Creator God. He said that if the 'gene map' for the human body were written down, the number of textbooks needed for all the information would reach the equivalent of a building eight stories high!

We are amazing creatures. One cannot fail to see the hand of a loving Creator in our design. The loving, personal God, who has stamped his personality on the world in creativity, I believe, is also the One who has left us the greatest legacy; that of individual gifts and talents. Each of your children is gifted in some special way, and your acceptance of, and love for, each of them will reflect God's love and approval of them.

We all need intimacy with other human beings—the knowledge that we are known and loved. But we also need "transcendence": the knowledge that we are loved by a Divine Being—someone who knows our name forever and is there when all else is gone. Our children need this especially. They are often more aware of the spiritual dimension to life than we are. So parents, don't forget to pray with your children. In an age when children are so exposed to violence and to scary entertainment, they need to know that their world is safe, that God's love is stronger than any evil they may have to face. Don't forget that to a little child, fathers are like "God with skin on!"

Fathers can leave a legacy of kindness, values and rich experience for their children. Or they can leave a different sort of legacy—one that is full of inappropriate anger, blame and sarcasm. These behaviours tend to become a pattern that is passed on to the children. Not because the fathers want to pass them on, but because the patterns become locked into the subconscious of their children's heads.

The title of this book assumes that men are prepared to take up the challenge. But if men are so brave, why is it that 80% of the people who seek help for relationship difficulties are women? It does take courage to get help when you need it. But it takes courage to eat curries, have vasectomies, play rugby and do all the other stuff that men do, too. So why can't we find the courage to do something really important for the sake of our children. I really encourage you to focus on what is important. I've had to do it. If you need some objective help in addressing anger or childhood issues, see it as a courageous step, not a sign of weakness.

Most of all Dads, do remember to look at the big picture. Don't get caught up in the performance trap, so that you have no energy left for your family.

At a recent seminar I attended, I watched as the presenter placed a large glass jar on the table. Beside the jar were a number of tennis ball-sized rocks. He asked the crowd, 'How many of these rocks do you think I can fit into this jar?' Someone guessed ten. Someone else guessed eight. The presenter began to place the rocks into the jar. Soon the jar filled up with a dozen or so rocks. The audience agreed that the jar was full. Then the presenter brought out a box of smaller rocks and poured them into the jar and they filtered down around the bigger rocks. He asked the audience, 'Is the jar full?'
'No!' they roared, because they knew what was next.
Sand! Then water!
'Now it's really full!'
The presenter asked, 'What's the point?'
Someone said, 'There is always room for more in your life!'
'Maybe,' said the presenter. 'But the point really is this. If the big rocks don't go in the jar first, they don't get in the jar at all!'
Great point!

Let's make sure we put the big rocks—relationships, family, and community—in our jars first! Let's make sure that in later years, we will be able to look back and know that we were true heroes—people who built people, not just people who built empires!

Remember, if you plant an acorn, you get an oak tree.

If we plant the seeds of great ideas in our children's hearts and minds, then we are likely to see great human beings.